Ben Pobjie is the author of *Error Australis*, *Mad Dogs and Thunderbolts* and *Second Best*, as well as countless articles about TV, sport, politics and the meaning of life scattered throughout the Australian media landscape. He lives in Sydney, where he spends his days panicking about deadlines.

100 TALES

from

AUSTRALIA'S *MOST* HAUNTED PLACES

BEN POBJIE

affirm
press

affirm press

First published by Affirm Press in 2022
This edition published in 2024
Bunurong/Boon Wurrung Country
28 Thistlethwaite Street
South Melbourne, VIC 3205
affirmpress.com.au

Affirm Press is located on the unceded land of the Bunurong/Boon Wurrung peoples
of the Kulin Nation. Affirm Press pays respect to their Elders past and present.

10 9 8 7 6 5 4 3 2 1

 A catalogue record for this
book is available from the
National Library of Australia

ISBN: 9781922992055 (mass market paperback)

Cover design by Josh Durham, Design by Committee
Image of Dagworth Station courtesy of the John Oxley Library,
State Library of Queensland
Image of George Ferguson Bowen courtesy of the Queensland
State Archives
Image of Adelaide Gaol courtesy of Adelaide Haunted Horizons
Image of Oakabella Homestead courtesy of Erik van Oost
Typeset in Minion Pro by J&M Typesetting
Printed and bound in China by C&C Offset Printing Co., Ltd.

 MIX
Paper | Supporting
responsible forestry
FSC® C008047

All reasonable effort has been made to attribute copyright and credit.
Any new information supplied will be included in subsequent editions.

To Freda, who keeps me safe from ghosts

Contents

Introduction

For as long as human beings have been dying, they have been turning into ghosts. Or maybe they haven't. That's the great thing about ghosts: nobody knows if they're real, so they are endlessly entertaining, like Bigfoot or Elon Musk.

Australian history is riddled with ghosts, which is unsurprising given that our nation's past is filled with violence and sadness and people dying in entertaining ways. Seemingly every country town has at least one ghost knocking about the place, lamenting his or her unfortunate demise and whipping up that peculiar mixture of terror and civic pride that only a local phantasm can produce.

Of course, some towns are more haunted than others, as this book will demonstrate. Kapunda in South Australia and Picton in New South Wales are great examples of hamlets with especially strong paranormal resonances, where the ectoplasm is particularly sticky and around every corner is another spook ready to startle you.

Not that every ghost is an unfriendly one. In these pages you will find ghosts of both the menacing and the kindly types, as well as plenty who have no real agenda beyond wandering in the hinterland between life and death, and making funny noises or giving off odd light.

Why do we love ghosts so much? Why do they fascinate us, obsess us, cause us to write books and songs and movies about them? Why, although we may be scared of them, do we simultaneously find ourselves so attracted to stories about them, and – let's be honest – hope that those stories are true?

Part of the answer is obvious: ghosts are evidence of life after death. Even the most ghastly ghost story carries within it a seed of hope: that when our body dies, perhaps our soul will carry on existing in some form. That form might be a blood-soaked nightmare stomping around the upper floor of an old pub and banging on innocent people's doors, but it's better than nothing.

But besides hope for ourselves, it's just plain exciting to imagine there is something beyond this world. The material realm is full of interesting stuff,* but it becomes even more thrilling if there's a whole other universe going on behind the scenes. To think that there could be an invisible presence brushing past you in a corridor; to believe that on a still, moonlit night you could catch sight of a mournful rider galloping through your town; to hope that the shadowy figure on the far side of the cemetery is a lost child from the 19th century and not just a bush … Who can resist the tantalising idea that our world has dimensions that our everyday experience only ever hints at?

In these pages you will come across a dizzying array of ghosts, spooks, phantoms, apparitions, unearthly presences and inexplicable encounters. You will meet tragic lovers, brutalised convicts, gruesome murder victims, unhappy children, miserable asylum inmates and their callous overseers, and even the odd esteemed politician. You will be taken all over Australia, from Queensland's blazing heat to the chilly greenery of Tasmania, from Western Australia's splendid isolation to the bustling streets of Melbourne and Sydney. You may believe all the stories contained herein, or you may not. But beyond a doubt, you will come away knowing that wherever the truth lies, there is indeed a hell of a lot of creepy stuff going on out there.

Dim the lights, hold tight to the hand of a loved one and make your way inside …

---

* The Taj Mahal, the A-Team et cetera.

Nurse Kerry

Ararat, Victoria

Nurses in mental asylums don't have a great reputation, thanks to *One Flew Over the Cuckoo's Nest*'s Nurse Ratched. But it turns out that if there's one thing scarier than a psychiatric nurse, it's a psychiatric nurse who has died but refuses to stop bossing you around. So it's no wonder that generations have had their spines chilled by Nurse Kerry, the stern overseer of Aradale Lunatic Asylum at Ararat, Victoria.

This grim, gigantic institution opened in 1867 and from the beginning operated as if its founders' primary aim was to provide a compelling backstory for a horror movie. The asylum was so huge that it was essentially a self-sufficient town in its own right, which was very convenient when it came to conducting controversial medical procedures well away from the prying eyes of the kind of fussy pedants who go around trying to shut hospitals down just because they specialise in lopping off bits of people's brains and shooting massive charges of electricity through them.

It took two signatures to commit someone to Aradale but eight to get someone released, meaning that only lunatics with a high friend-to-enemy ratio ever got out. About 13,000 people died within Aradale's forbidding walls, so it is no surprise that the place is said to be crawling with ghosts, most of whom combine severe mental illness with a well-justified grudge against society. They are not, in other words, the kind of ghosts you want to take on a picnic.

But the most unnerving phantom of all those resident at Aradale is undoubtedly Nurse Kerry. This conscientious healthcare professional has been spotted by many of the tourists who nowadays pass through the cold corridors of the asylum, her footsteps heard clacking up and down the halls and her starched white uniform a common sight as she makes sure all is in order.

Aradale was closed down in 1998, but Kerry, obviously seeing how tough the job market was for older women, opted to stay on and continue the smooth running of the organisation. Given the buildings are reportedly swarming with unstable and unfriendly spirits, one might think it was almost a comfort to have Kerry around to keep the inmates under control and protect innocent members of the public. However, the impression the nurse gives is not so much a protective one as that she is keen to add those innocent members of the public to the register of patients. Visitors to the electro-shock room report a hot buzzing in the temples, the machinery apparently eager to get back to business. And with Nurse Kerry always watching over you, it's hard to escape the feeling that she's eager to strap you down herself.

This is far from the only symptom reported by guests of the asylum. Those who wander into the areas once used for lobotomies claim to suffer intense headaches, which suggests that the staff continue to hang around and do their best, with limited ghostly resources, to keep performing the procedures. Other visitors to the facility report nausea, which is not necessarily a paranormal phenomenon but definitely in sync with the general vibe.

More disturbing, unless you've had a big lunch, are the women's screams that can be heard echoing throughout the corridors of the asylum, and the shadowy figures seen flitting between rooms and around corners. With the misery inflicted on thousands in the place – operations frequently done without anaesthesia, and patients treated less as unfortunate people suffering from serious illness than as unusually large flies under the care of scientists writing papers on the implications of wing detachment – one can assume that very few of those scuttling around the hallways or crying out in the night are happy souls.

Whether they are screaming for relief, begging for mercy, bent on revenge or simply howling in pain, you can be sure they are under the tender loving care of Nurse Kerry. And, should you take the wrong corner on a ghost tour, maybe you will be too.

Behind Adelaide's Bars

Adelaide, South Australia

A feeling that you're being watched. Footsteps behind you. Voices in the distance. A hand emerging from an empty cell to slam the slot in the door shut. Adelaide Gaol has all sorts of treats in store for mortals who like to get close to spooks. It opened in 1841, when the South Australian governor realised that not being a penal colony doesn't guarantee you won't have any criminals, and operated right up until 1988. That's a lot of time to accumulate stories, and Adelaide Gaol has some great ones.

Ben Ellis was the prison's hangman for ten years in the 19th century, and was known as an exceedingly fine one. He had a flawless record of carrying out executions quickly, cleanly and without undue suffering … well, *almost* flawless. When hanging the murderer Charles Streitman, he got careless. Streitman, not properly prepared by Ellis, dropped, bounced and got caught on the platform. It took him twenty-two agonising minutes to die.

In 1873, Ellis had to hang Elizabeth Woolcock, the only woman ever executed in South Australia. Elizabeth may or may not have been guilty of poisoning her husband, who had violently abused her for years. The death of Elizabeth, just twenty-five years old, shook the hangman and caused him to reflect deeply on his job, and his purpose. Today, Ben Ellis's ghost walks regularly through Adelaide Gaol, unable to keep still, hoping somehow to beg for forgiveness for the deadly efficiency with which he carried out his task for so long.

The first governor of Adelaide Gaol was William Baker Ashton, a large, spherical man who'd once been a police sergeant in London. His rotund, jolly-looking form suited his reputation for showing kindness and generosity to the inmates at Adelaide. Every year he paid for Christmas dinner for the prisoners out of his own pocket; the gaol became known as 'Ashton's Hotel' thanks to his compassionate treatment. But the merry fat man was laid low by allegations of corruption and drunkenness, and by the time he was cleared by the courts it was three months too late: Ashton had died of a heart attack.

Ashton also haunts the gaol where he once worked, unable to get any rest due to the dreadful injustice under which he died. On stormy nights he can be heard in his old office, moving around non-existent furniture.

And then there's Frederick Carr. Fred was hanged on 12 November 1929 for the murder of his wife, Maud, who had been found in bed with her throat cut. The case against Fred was strong, but he protested his innocence to the last. 'The law requires my body, but it cannot have my soul, as I am innocent,' he said. Nevertheless, he met his end by the noose.

By the stairs of the New Building of Adelaide Gaol, Fred Carr is a regular sight. Well dressed and cordial, he is reported to be far from an angry or vengeful spirit, despite the death he considered unjust. Indeed, those who've met him say he seems motivated more by friendly curiosity than anything else, simply enjoying meeting new people and taking an interest in them. As prison ghosts go, he is one of the more amiable.

The oddest thing about Fred Carr's ghost – and the thing that, despite his cheerful demeanour, could be said to make him just a *little* bit terrifying – is that he used to appear without a face. Well turned out, certainly, and well spoken, too – but minus a face. Until, that is, November of the year 2000, when he was seen with face present and correct and, moreover, sporting a big smile. Fred's face was back, and he was quite chuffed by the development.

Why did Fred Carr go faceless for seventy-three years after his death, and why was it suddenly restored to him? Nobody knows, and it seems likely nobody will ever know. It's just another mystery that lives within the walls of the old Adelaide Gaol.

The Young and Jackson Hotel

Melbourne, Victoria

Young and Jackson's is a Melbourne institution. Established in 1861 on the corner of Flinders and Swanston streets, across the road from the grandeur of Flinders Street Station, it continues to do a bustling trade with thirsty locals, commuters and tourists alike. One of its most famous attractions is *Chloé*, a painting of an attractive and unclothed young lady by Jules Joseph Lefebvre. After creating an uproar in late-1800s Australian society, which was scandalised by the hitherto unsuspected revelation that women have nipples, the demure maiden was purchased by the hotel and has hung in the bar ever since.

There is, however, an even more intriguing young woman associated with the pub. If she is less likely to cause an uproar at an exhibition, this lady is certainly more apt to turn your hair white if you happen to run into her while dropping in for a schooner after work.

With a history dating back to the Victorian gold rush, in the days when Melbourne was a wild and rowdy town whose citizens engaged in the noble traditions of – depending on social status – drunken disorder and moralistic tongue-clicking as enthusiastically as any upright denizens of a colonial frontier town, the Young and Jackson Hotel has played host to some colourful characters – and some macabre deeds. Evidence of the latter can be witnessed on certain dark nights by a lamppost outside the hotel's doors.

It is here, leaning against that post, that you can see a lovely young woman, perhaps waiting for a late-night rendezvous, perhaps on her way home from one. Wherever she is headed, there is no doubt that she is uncommonly beautiful. Attired in elegant Victorian garb, she might be a tourist attraction in herself – in fact, one might easily believe her to be an employee of Young and Jackson's, hired to promote the hotel as a destination of historical significance and old-world charm.

You may feel compelled to approach her, to get a better look at her loveliness, or perhaps with a chivalrous urge to offer assistance as she stands lonely and winsome in the pool of light. Perhaps you sense a beckoning in her gaze. You would be well advised to resist, however, for as you get closer you will become aware of a detail that was not at first apparent: this beautiful young lady standing in the lamplight has had her throat slit from ear to ear. The shocking red slash glints in the light like a clown's grin, as her despairing eyes lock onto yours and her mouth opens in a silent cry.*

Who is this unhappy young woman? Nobody knows. Just one of the hundreds of thousands who have passed in and out of Young and Jackson's over the decades; doubtless she is not the only one who met a tragic fate on the dark and dangerous city streets. If she wants anything from us, she either can't or won't let us know. She simply stands there, watching the people go by, striking terror into the hearts of anyone foolish enough to seek a closer look at her pretty countenance just by displaying the gruesome fact of her demise. As Chloé hangs inside, the object of admiration and adoration by the masses, she languishes outside, alone and forgotten, but determined to find someone to remind.

If she has any message to give to us, perhaps it is just that, if you've had a big night at Young and Jackson's, you should not linger on your way home – for outside the bubble of bonhomie and warmth lies a cold trail of lonely blood.

---

* You probably won't see this bit, of course, as you'll already be running frantically in the opposite direction.

Ghosts of Port Arthur

Port Arthur, Tasmania

You don't have to try hard to sense the ghosts of the Port Arthur Historic Site. The former denizens of the old convict settlement close in around you, insistent and suffocating, as soon as you arrive. If you can't see or hear them, you can feel them: the souls of thousands of the tortured, the abused and the murdered. The very air is weighted and perfumed with the pain and anger and sadness of a place built specifically to inflict those very things.

Port Arthur was where the British Empire sent the 'worst of the worst' of its convicts, and where the worst of the worst punishments were carried out. There were floggings and hangings, but it was also a place where authorities experimented with more innovative punishments. Like the 'Silent System', which sought to reform the criminal character through sensory deprivation. The convict had a hood placed over his head and was kept in solitary confinement for twenty-three hours a day, in a room with soundproofed walls. On Sundays, they went to church with masks on. With no light and no sound, many prisoners went mad – just another string to Port Arthur's hellish bow.

Walking through Port Arthur – the prison, the lunatic asylum, the Commandant's House – one can feel the jostling of desperate spirits, yoked to the site that broke them. The 'worst of the worst' they were – except that some were far from hardened criminals. Among the brutes and the monsters were the mentally ill, the plain unlucky, the men who had pushed back against the wrong warden at their last prison. In some cases they were children: boys as young as nine were sent to Port Arthur. Some have been spotted more lately there, standing at windows, staring out and lurking in corners of the old sleeping quarters.

Some of the most fearsome hauntings can be found in the punishment cells at the 'Separate Prison', those dark, noiseless dungeons where the Silent System was enacted. In these cells, where men were kept for as long as thirty days, many visitors have felt hands upon them when they entered. Some have had their throats gripped; on occasion, red scratches appear. Others have been grabbed or pushed. The cells are small and, after all these years, apparently crowded with spirits.

The ghosts of Port Arthur are inescapable. At the Commandant's House, lights swing back and forth without a breath of wind, an old woman sits in a rocking chair and children run between rooms. At the old asylum, voices mutter and moan, chains clank and floorboards creak with no one walking upon them. In the prison complex, living visitors feel invisible inmates brush against them and occasionally whisper in their ears.

Today, people travel to Port Arthur specifically to see ghosts. They step into the punishment cells hoping to be pummelled or thrown against a wall. They wander through the halls hoping to hear the voices of doomed men cry out to them. They turn cameras up to the windows hoping to see the sad faces of children looking back at them. They cross their fingers that, while they are there, a cold wind will blow through the old prison and set the fittings rattling. It's one way of finding the silver lining.

One thing is for sure: the ghosts at Port Arthur are not the happy sort. The poltergeists are not playful. The spectres do not smile on visitors. When you feel the icy fingers of the prison's phantoms close around your wrist or tug on your clothes, they are not reaching out to make friends. These ghosts are the lonely echoes of atrocity, grasping frantically at whoever and whatever passes by them, in the hope that there's a way out of the endless torment in which they are trapped.

There never is. Two centuries and more of misery are woven into the fabric of Port Arthur, and while the tourists come and go, and snap their photographs, the ghosts continue to mourn their own suffering.

Room 302

Brisbane, Queensland

They call it Room 302, the small collection of rooms deep within Brisbane's City Hall. Why do 'they' call it Room 302 when it comprises several rooms rather than one? Is it because they saw *The Shining* and realised it was way cooler for a haunting to occur in a specific room with a specific number, rather than, say, 'It happened in a small collection of rooms'? There's no way to be sure, because nobody knows who 'they' are. 'They' are a secretive bunch, and god knows what 'they' get up to when we're not looking. But all this is beside the point, which is …

That the little group of rooms in City Hall *is* called Room 302, and it's a spooky enough name for a spooky enough place. It was once used as a darkroom, which is one of the spookiest uses for a room to have, what with the darkness and the menacing red lighting and the ever-present possibility that as you're hanging up the new prints you will spot something terrifying in the corner of one of the photos, something shocking, something that chills you to the bone and yet, at the same time, causes the whole horrible business to make a dreadful, sickening kind of sense, something that …

You take my point. But Room 302 was spooky even before people started soaking paper in magic water that made amazing images appear from nowhere. It was in the 1950s that the stories started to be heard from the good workers of the Brisbane City Council.

Stories of sudden blasts of cold air – hitherto unknown in Brisbane. Stories of footsteps – which had hitherto been known in Brisbane but were slightly unusual, because they were being heard in places where there weren't any feet.

And most of all, stories of a *presence*. It's hard to define exactly what a presence is, but it's like pornography: you know it when you see it. Or rather, when you don't see it. A presence isn't seen or heard, it is felt. The air becoming heavier, a buzzing in your head, a strange and oppressive sensation that you are being watched. It's an *energy*, one that makes the hair on the back of your neck stand on end and your flesh crawl. It's the utter conviction that you're not alone, even when you are. It's feeling like you're the girl who's gone down to the basement to investigate a weird noise, and the music is getting really tense. And what's worse: you're only in your underwear and you're not a virgin.

That's how people felt when they went into Room 302, and there was a perfectly reasonable explanation for that – and by 'perfectly reasonable', I mean 'horrible'.

As I mentioned, it was in the 1950s that people began to sense the oppressive horror of Room 302 and hear the phantom footsteps. And it was in the 1940s that the source of that horror could be found. For it was then that a caretaker in Brisbane City Hall had become so fed up with the low pay and the long hours and the loneliness and the terrible state of his marriage and the absence of really high-quality cultural pursuits in South East Queensland at the time that he gave up the ghost.

Or rather, he did the exact opposite of giving up the ghost: he killed himself, which actually brought the ghost into being. And though he never showed himself to anyone visually, he let everyone know he was there, trapped mournfully in the bowels of City Hall by the act he'd hoped would release him from the world for good.

The caretaker's successors in the role eventually took action: after years of reports of the nightmarish quality of Room 302, that section of the building was sealed shut, so as to prevent the scarification of staff going about their daily business. Which was all well and good, but if you wanted to protect people from spooks at Brisbane City Hall, you'd have to do better than shutting up Room 302. But that's another story …

The Pearl Buyer of Broome

Broome, Western Australia

As a rule, the mainstream Christian religions are quite strict when it comes to which ghosts are real and which aren't. The Holy Ghost, for example: real. Patrick Swayze in the film *Ghost*: not real. Thus it was that the first Anglican bishop of North West Australia, Gerard Trower – a man who already had his share of troubles, what with his job title being so unwieldy – suffered quite a shock when he moved into the Bishop's Palace in Broome and found himself with a somewhat disconcerting housemate.

Late one night, early in his residence, Bishop Trower awoke to find his bedroom awash with an unearthly light. The illumination emanated from a man who had, rather impolitely, entered his bedchamber without so much as a by-your-leave. The bishop would later describe him as being dressed in a rabbi's garb, which must've only added to the complicated religious questions the apparition was causing Trower to contemplate.

The ghostly rabbi didn't speak or interact with the bedroom's current resident. He simply strolled about as if he owned the place, for which there was quite a good explanation: once upon a time, he had.

The man seen by Bishop Trower was Abraham de Vahl Davis, and the story of how he ended up in the bishop's bedroom – in a state that could be described as less than optimally corporeal – is also the story of Australia's worst ever civilian maritime disaster.

The SS *Koombana* is known as 'Australia's *Titanic*': not just for the incredibly luxurious nature of the ship itself, nor for the appalling loss of life its sinking brought about, nor for the incredible popularity of its theme song. For the *Koombana*, like the *Titanic*, sank in 1912. In fact, it sank around 20 March, nearly a month before the *Titanic* – so if anything, the *Titanic* should be known as 'Britain's *Koombana*', and it's only racism that means it isn't. But I digress.

When the *Koombana* sank north of Port Hedland, Abraham de Vahl Davis was on board, and in possession of a rather special item: the fabled Roseate Pearl. The history of this pearl was a bloody and sordid one, and exactly the kind of thing that generally ends up with ghosts in bishops' bedrooms.

The Roseate Pearl was a pearl of uncommon size and beauty, which got its name from the fact that it was both a pearl and roseate. It was discovered by a West Australian pearl diver many years earlier, but had been stolen from him by a fellow diver, in a scene very reminiscent of the theft of the One Ring from Déagol by Sméagol in JRR Tolkien's *The Lord of the Rings*.* The pearl was later taken from the second diver by two Chinese gangsters, who were then hanged for murder – the murder being unrelated to the pearl. Or was it? The pearl was acquiring a reputation for bringing misery and woe to whoever held it – again, very Tolkien – and it's hard to say whether any misfortune was truly 'unrelated'.

After the execution of the Chinese men, the Roseate Pearl was sold to an unfortunate fellow who promptly suffered a fatal heart attack, and then passed to an even less fortunate fellow who had the pearl stolen from him and then killed himself. You'll begin to sense the pattern. The pearl, in a nutshell,† was bad news. In 1905 it came into the possession of the pearl dealer Mark Liebglid, who was subsequently

---

* If that helps you picture it.

† Or oyster shell, more pertinently.

found facedown in the ocean off Broome, and not recreationally – he'd been bashed to death and thrown into the water.

The pearl continued its haphazard trail of destruction, being sold by a Filipino man to finance his voyage home. The Filipino died as soon as he got there, and the man he sold it to committed suicide after the pearl was stolen from him. By now all this was getting kind of monotonous, so it's no wonder the pearl decided to change things up a little.

Abraham de Vahl Davis, a prosperous pearl dealer who also liked to moonlight as a rabbi for reasons that, through the mists of history, aren't that easy to discern, bought the Roseate Pearl for £20,000* in Port Hedland and hopped on the SS *Koombana*, bound for his home in Broome.

But he never got there. Not in physical form, anyway. Like everyone else on board the *Koombana*, he went to the bottom of the Indian Ocean. Like no one else on board the *Koombana*, though, he did make it home in his own way. For the Bishop's Palace had once been Davis's own house, so it was no wonder he wound up wandering around it in his rabbi's gear; clearly, Bishop Trower had caught Davis on one of his more spiritual evenings, causing the old man severe ecumenical palpitations.

And his spectral presence, without explanation, left open one of Australia's greatest mysteries: did the Roseate Pearl even exist?

That's right. For all the tragedy and woe that it wrought, for all the death and destruction that accompanied it, nobody knows whether this legendary pearl was actually a thing. And most likely we never will, for if it did exist, it's been returned to the sea whence it came, and the only one who knows the truth is a transparent rabbi stalking the halls of the Bishop's Palace, wondering where it all went wrong.

---

* In today's terms, between $8 and $14.

The Phantom of Government House

Hobart, Tasmania

Government House, Hobart, is an imposing old pile. Built in the 1850s, it possesses a grandeur that almost seems a bit out of character for Tasmania, the gingerbread cottage of Australian states. From its sweeping lawns and fountains to its stunning stonework and intricately carved gargoyles, to its spectacular ballroom and elegant drawing room, it is the very picture of colonial splendour.

No doubt Admiral Sir Thomas Hugh Binney, KCB, KCMG, DSO,[*] thought it a most fitting residence when he and his wife, Elizabeth, moved in on Christmas Eve 1945. The governorship of Tasmania was a marvellous Christmas present for the admiral, who had served with distinction in the Royal Navy before settling down to a quiet life of doing whatever it is that governors do.[†]

But as pretty much always happens when people move into a big fancy house, shit started getting weird as soon as convenient.

The first inkling that the grand Gothic Revival mansion might be having a Gothic revival came when the houseman[‡] George Heron caught sight of ... something at the end of a long hallway. That's another problem with these big houses: long hallways. They make it difficult

---

[*] I know, it's a bit much, isn't it?

[†] Brace yourself: it's not a lot.

[‡] A houseman is a vice-regal position in a governor's household that is best defined as 'a man who is in a house'.

20

to know exactly what you've seen walking briskly across a doorway down the other end of one. Heron was never sure what he'd spied in that hallway, but there was absolutely no doubt that it was possible he might've definitely seen a potential ghost. For sure.

Heron's vision could just have been written off as one of those crazy hallucinations so typical of the average houseman, had not spooky doings continued to make themselves known. One evening, Lady Binney saw the faithful Heron walking down a corridor. Which would not be a big deal normally, except that the faithful Heron was, at the time, downstairs in the kitchen. Who did Lady Binney see? Someone else who worked at the house? Okay, that is possible – but it's still weird, right? How many times must people see people wandering halls where there are no people before people say, 'Yeah, nah, ghost'? More than twice?

The question is moot, because if the fleeting sightings of hall-walkers weren't enough, the eeriness of Government House was about to move into high gear.

One night Lady Binney was kicking around the house, perhaps having donned some comfy trackie daks, when she did what people of the post-war period frequently did in their own homes: she walked from one room into another.

The room was empty, to begin with. There is no doubt whatsoever about that. Lady Binney had just been in there, and she knew for a fact that there was not a single soul in that room. Or, at least, there was not a single *body* in that room. Whether there was a single soul was a question that became a lot more complicated when Lady Binney heard, clear as a bell, a voice ringing out loudly and confidently. A voice that cried, 'A quarter past eleven!'

And that was the eerie thing …

For the fact is, *it was not a quarter past eleven*. It was, in fact, only just gone ten.

Lady Binney was paralysed with terror. Disembodied voices were one thing, but what possible reason could any spectral presence have for deliberately misleading people as to the correct time? What dark business did this phantom have that required residents of Government House to believe it was seventy-five minutes later than it really was? One shudders to imagine, as Lady Binney did on that dreadful night when she came face to non-face with this malevolent and chronologically misleading spirit.

The mystery of the ghost of Government House has never been resolved, and he has remained in that room, calling out the wrong time, over the decades. Some believe that if he ever calls out 'A quarter past eleven' when it actually *is* a quarter past eleven, his restless soul will finally be at peace, and he will fade from the earthly realm. Others believe that this is nonsense that some idiot just made up. But whatever the truth of the Hobart phantasm – be he deceased former governor, unlucky home invader or simply a passer-by with a broken watch – he's certainly one of the most interesting things ever to happen in Tasmania.

The Liftman

Brisbane, Queensland

The elevator in Brisbane City Hall was notorious for mechanical difficulties. It would become stuck between floors. The doors would malfunction. On more than one occasion, fires broke out in the lift well. The problems started back in the 1930s. The culprit, they said, was the ghostly liftman who rode the elevator.

On 31 October 1935 – Halloween, as it happened – George Edward Betts left his Bardon home at 7am. He cheerfully bade his wife farewell, kissing her on the cheek and mentioning that he'd be dropping in to see the doctor on his way to work.[*] A building contractor, George Betts was working on a construction project. He arrived on site and worked through the morning. At lunchtime, he changed his clothes and told his workmates that he had to head into the city. This was no surprise – he had already indicated that he had to visit City Hall to pay for a water connection at another site he'd been working on.

They say it is the ghost of a lift operator who committed suicide, or perhaps died in a ghastly accident, jumping from the clock tower of City Hall, or being crushed by his own elevator. Ever since, they say, he rides the lift and causes trouble.

At 2.15pm, City Hall lift attendant George Jones welcomed two people into his lift and took them up to the observation landing at the

---

[*]   Did his wife ask why? Apparently not. An oddly incurious woman.

top of the tower. One was a woman whose name remains unknown. The other was George Edward Betts. As far as George Jones could tell, the two were strangers to each other. Five minutes after they had exited the lift, George Jones let the woman back on and took her down to the ground floor. For a few minutes, George Betts was left alone at the top of the tower.

Many years later, when the clock tower was being renovated, a construction worker saw the silhouette of a man standing in an area where the public was not allowed. On investigation, no one was there.

Shortly after the lift descended from the observation landing, the inhabitants of City Hall were startled by a colossal crash. They rushed to find the source of the noise, and discovered a hole in the building's iron roof. Finding the room beneath the hole, the searchers came across the body of George Betts. He had fallen forty metres from the observation landing, crashed through the roof and slammed into the little room's concrete floor.

Although stories of the ghostly liftman abounded, and that unfortunate former employee was long blamed for the strange happenings in that elevator, no record of any lift operator dying in City Hall, by suicide or otherwise, can be found.

After the tragic accident, an inquest was held into George Betts's death. Evidence was provided that there was nothing wrong with the safety railing on the observation landing, and the only way anyone could have fallen over it was if they had climbed up on the railing to look at something. Or if they had gone over it on purpose.

The ghost in the City Hall tower is still riding the lift.

Nobody ever discovered why George Betts went to the doctor that morning.

The Huntsman of Rostrevor

Rostrevor, South Australia

Francis Grote was a noble man, which is not quite the same thing as a nobleman: indeed, often the two are directly opposed. Nonetheless, though not an aristocrat, Francis Grote was a man of some standing: he was one of nine brothers of the English historian George Grote, after whom Grote Street in Adelaide was named, and a trustee of St George's Church at Woodforde. Francis had come to Campbelltown, just north of Adelaide, in 1854, and settled in the house called Orange Grove, in the district of Rostrevor.

Of all the Australian colonies, South Australia was perhaps the best suited for those who wished to re-create the genteel life of a gentleman back in England, and Orange Grove was a charming place in which to be English. Being a keen sportsman, Francis Grote happily gave use of his land to the Adelaide Hunt, which was dedicated to advancing the cause of Western civilisation in the furthest outposts of empire by ensuring there was a place a man could go to chase a fox to exhaustion and watch it be torn to pieces by dogs. Through such elite recreations did the proud Englishman demonstrate just how civilised he was.

Francis Grote's Rostrevor property became quite a centre of fox-hunting activity and thereby of Adelaide society. Many grand hunts were held at Orange Grove, accompanied by elegant balls at which the most extravagantly bedecked ladies of Adelaide would dance with the suavest gentlemen, complimenting them on the glossiness of their moustaches and the elan with which they killed the wild animals that had been imported from England for that express purpose.

Grote himself was one of the most enthusiastic and impressive huntsmen of all. No Adelaide gentleman ever looked more dashing in his red coat and black helmet, astride his proud charger. No sportsman ever more charismatically smeared his face with fox blood. But his days of hunting were growing short.

For Francis Grote was sick. His illness was chronic and incurable and caused him terrible pain. Life, even for an Englishman in the suburbs of Adelaide with a steady supply of foxes and social functions, became drained of value. The pain overwhelming and the prospect of living out his days in agony unacceptable, on 23 December 1867 he gave himself an early Christmas present: an overdose of laudanum.

Under the laws of the time, suicide, or *felo-de-se* ('felon of himself' in Latin) was a crime equivalent to murder, and they didn't even put the Lifeline number at the bottom of newspaper articles about it. At the inquest into Grote's death, he was found posthumously guilty of murdering himself, the sentence being the seizure of his property by the government. In earlier years he would have been buried at a crossroads with a stake through his heart, the authorities having confused suicide with vampires.* In the marginally less mental time of the 1860s, he was simply denied a Christian burial, being interred at night between 9pm and midnight without any religious ceremony. Given he was already dead, the punishment seems to lack bite, but it was still kind of mean.

Francis Grote, however, most likely did not give two figs for what they did to him after death, because his suicide had indubitably set him free. Free from the pain that had racked his body and prevented him from truly savouring life. Death, too, could be said to throw a spanner in the works, life-savouring-wise, but that would be reckoning without the enormous opportunities of being a ghost.

For once Francis Grote released himself from the mortal plane, the

---

* They actually used to do this. Freaking weirdos, right?

ghost huntsman began his joyous rides through the fields and paddocks around Orange Grove. Illness had curtailed his life on the hunt, but in death the hunt could go on forever, the ghostly rider on his ghostly horse, phantom hounds at his heels, ceaselessly chasing a spectral fox. Those who have seen the huntsman of Rostrevor, his transparent form galloping through the land that once was his, have seen a soul freed, and a spirit at peace, and at home.

The Broken Heart of Oyster Harbour

Oyster Harbour, Western Australia

It was in Ireland that Catherine Spense met Cathal and fell in love, and soon enough the two were married. Together they were happy but poor, and so Catherine and Cathal crossed the sea to England in the hope of finding better fortunes there. But better fortunes they did not find, and a desperate Cathal turned to thievery to keep himself and his young bride alive. Sadly, he was no great shakes at the thieving business, and soon enough he was caught, and soon enough he was sentenced, and almost as soon as that he was clapped in irons, put on a boat and taken off to Australia for ten long, sad years.

Catherine was despondent at her true love's transportation, but she was also a clever and courageous woman, and so allowed herself only a moment's moping before setting out to turn things around. In defiance of the fact that it was the 1860s and she was, blatantly, a woman, young Catherine marched out and got herself a job. Working for a wealthy lawyer, she impressed with her infinite resourcefulness and sagacity – and if she impressed him in any other respects, or with the performance of tasks not strictly office-related, it is frankly none of our business. The point is she made herself completely indispensable to the old fellow.

Meanwhile, Cathal was also hard at work on a chain gang in Western Australia, and as sad as a man could ever be. Bereft at being torn from his home and the woman he loved and taken to the end of the

Earth to haul stone for the tyrannical British, his anguish was multiplied by the fact that, as he was completely illiterate, he could not write home to let his wife know where he was or even that he was still alive.

But Catherine never lost faith that she would one day be reunited with her beloved Cathal, and in 1877 her faith was rewarded when the rich lawyer fortuitously dropped dead. In recognition of that indispensability I mentioned earlier, he had left her a large sum: large enough, in fact, for her to book passage on a ship to Australia. Which she did forthwith, though she did not know exactly where her husband was, or indeed whether he was alive. But Catherine was gutsy and determined, and still, after all those years, in love: she would not be stopped by mere uncertainty. So it was that after many months she arrived in Albany and began making enquiries.

Catherine was told by a local priest that there was a man living across the bay, at Oyster Harbour, who might well be her long-lost husband. On Catherine's behalf, the priest went to visit this man, who revealed that he was indeed Cathal, and who was overjoyed to hear his lady love was nearby. 'Tell my wife,' he said to the priest, 'that I shall catch a boat across the harbour in two days' time. I shall meet her on the shore at twilight.'

Catherine's heart leaped when the priest returned with the message. After ten years of sadness and longing, she was to be reunited with her beloved!* Two days later, as the sun set over the Indian Ocean, Catherine stood silhouetted against the red sky and watched as the boat carrying Cathal drew nearer.

The boat was no more than a few hundred yards from shore when Cathal spotted his wife waiting by the water. Overcome with the euphoria of love restored, the unlucky Irishman stood up to wave to Catherine – and tipped the boat over. As his beloved watched from the shore, Cathal flailed, struggled and sank beneath the waves. After ten years of waiting, he had perished just a stone's throw from a happy reunion.

---

* I know, you can see where this is going …

Catherine let out a wail that carried for miles. Her heart suddenly shattered, she collapsed to the ground, all life drained from her in that one terrible instant. She was carried to shelter and attempts were made to revive her, but to no avail. Catherine Spense, having worked for ten years and then crossed the globe to be with her one true love, had died of a broken heart.

And ever since, even to this day, when the air is still around Oyster Bay, you can still hear Catherine's lovelorn wail, and see her ghostly form walking sadly by the shore up and down Seamen's Walk. Forever walking, forever weeping, forever hoping that somehow, someday, she and her precious Cathal might be together again.

The Visitor of Bulimba

Bulimba, Queensland

The seemingly humble Brisbane suburb of Bulimba has many claims to fame. It's where Queensland's first locally built bicycle was constructed, for example. And ... many other things. But the jewel in Bulimba's crown is Bulimba House, a stately home that got its name from the fact it was in Bulimba and it was a house. The town of Bulimba itself grew up around the house, and for the best part of two centuries it has been the area's main attraction, particularly for one extremely persistent local.

Because for nearly two centuries, someone has been desperate to get into Bulimba House, and they just won't give up.

Bulimba House was built by – or at least built for – the innovative pastoralist David McConnel and his wife, Mary, who founded Brisbane's first children's hospital. If you were a fan of sick children or lucerne, they were a real power couple in colonial Queensland. They showed their progressive streak by naming the house Bulimba, after the local Aboriginal name for the area, meaning 'place of the magpie lark', and their non-progressive streak by taking over and farming on the local Aboriginal people's land. Was it the white man's disrespect for the original inhabitants of Bulimba that saw the house cursed by invisible presences? Probably not, but it would be a neat story if it were, wouldn't it? Really wrap things up nicely and provide a moral to the whole thing.

31

As it is, it's a mystery that defies easy explanation, for from early on in the life of Bulimba House, the same thing has kept on happening. The dogs begin to bark and the servants scurry to answer a powerful and insistent knocking at the front door. It could happen at noon or at midnight or at four in the morning, but it is always an urgent knocking, the knocking of someone with a very good reason for wanting to get into the house. Though it must be said that since they always knock, they are presumably also reasonably well mannered: nobody has ever reported hearing rocks thrown at windows or the door being kicked.

When the knocking came, the door was answered, but always with the same result: nobody was there. The McConnels, in their time at Bulimba House, never saw the person who was so desirous of paying them a visit. Over the years, many other prominent people took up residence at Bulimba. Fellow pastoralist Donald Coutts bought it from the McConnels and subdivided the property, but still the visitor came to demand entry. In 1935, the house was purchased by former Queensland premier Arthur Edward Moore, and the knocking kept coming, and still nobody was seen.

Who knows why the knocker comes, or why he or she needs so badly to get in? Perhaps when the house was first built, there came a dark and stormy night, and a fugitive running desperately through the howling wind and the hammering rain. Perhaps that person swam the Brisbane River with some dreadful pursuit close behind and, on seeing the lights of the grand house on the hill, thought sanctuary awaited.

Perhaps they climbed the hill and banged on the door, begging to be heard and to be saved. Perhaps, as the lightning split the black sky and the thunder crashed all around, their knocking and their cries went unheard ... or heard, but ignored. And perhaps, on the doorstep of Bulimba House, whatever was chasing that unhappy individual caught up with them, and they met a grim and ghastly fate, all because the rich folk inside could not or would not answer the call for sanctuary.

Perhaps it is that lonely fugitive, soaked to the bone and exhausted beyond reason, who to this day pounds out judgement on the front door of Bulimba House, doomed in death to cry out for the hospitality they never received in life.

Fisher's Ghost

Campbelltown, New South Wales

John Farley burst into the Campbelltown Hotel, eyes wild and breaths coming in panicked gasps. He had run all the way from the creek to tell the men of the town the baffling and bloodcurdling sight he had just seen.

'I saw Fred Fisher,' he stammered breathlessly, '*sitting on the bridge*.'

As Farley had expected, the pub patrons responded with a level of scornful incredulity. For Frederick Fisher had left Campbelltown four months previously to return to his native England.

Yet Farley knew what he had seen, and he told the crowd exactly that: Fred Fisher was seated on the rail of the bridge. But that was not the end of the chilling tale, for in the gloom of the evening, Fisher had glowed with an eerie light, and Farley saw blood dripping from a terrible wound on his head. Turning towards the petrified passer-by, Fisher emitted an unearthly, wordless moan, raised a bony finger and pointed to the paddock by the creek. This indication made, he vanished.

The incredulity did not become less scornful at this detail. Was Farley claiming he had seen a *ghost*? Come now. This might've been the 19th century, but the men of Campbelltown – then a remote frontier hamlet at the outermost limits of the white man's incursions into New South Wales – were not complete idiots. After all, could they not remember clearly the day Fred Fisher had left: 17 June 1826?

Had they not seen with their own eyes Fisher's friend and neighbour George Worrall assuring them that the young farmer had gone back to England? Had they not heard with their own ears Worrall saying that, before leaving, Fisher had given his pal Worrall power of attorney over his property? Were they not right there on the scene when Worrall let everyone know that Fisher had written to him to say he wasn't coming back and that Worrall could have his farm? Had they not ...

Okay, maybe it couldn't hurt to have a quick look in that paddock.

The fact that Fisher had disappeared without a trace and there was only one man's testimony to rely on as regards his movements and destination had not aroused any suspicion till now: apparently, what was needed to really spark the locals' curiosity was a ghost sighting. The police had a snoop around the paddock and, to the dismay and horror of all, found Frederick Fisher's remains buried by the side of the creek – just where, according to John Farley, the man's ghost had pointed that dread day.

George Worrall, the man who had taken over Fisher's farm, claimed ownership of his horses and who, for some reason, had started to go around wearing Fisher's clothes was, perhaps unsurprisingly, immediately arrested. He confessed to Fisher's murder and was hanged, and thus was the story ended.

Except not really, because the tale of Fisher's ghost, sitting on the rail, pointing out his earthly remains, caught the imagination of the world like few do. Poems, songs, books, plays, an opera and a movie have drawn inspiration from Fisher. Charles Dickens himself wrote a version of the story. And to this day, every November, Campbelltown celebrates the Fisher's Ghost Festival,* an event which brings together the whole town to celebrate community and ghosts. There are fireworks, a parade, an art award, a fun run and lots of other things that, if you lived in Campbelltown, might seem like appealing leisure activities.

For a ghost who is recorded as having appeared just once, to one

---

*   It lasts for ten days. Seems a bit much, doesn't it?

man, Frederick Fisher certainly has cast a long shadow.[*] If he returned to the earthly realm to seek justice, perhaps he attained it with Worrall's execution, and therefore now rests in peace. Or perhaps, by what is now known as Fisher's Ghost Creek, he can still, on a dark night, if you pass at the right time, be seen, turning his pale and bloody visage on you and pointing out murder by the light of his own uncanny glow.

---

[*] Do ghosts cast shadows? Remind me to check this.

The Murdering Sandhills

Narrandera, New South Wales

By the banks of the Murrumbidgee, about fifteen kilometres north-west of Narrandera, can be found the serene spot that goes by the extremely un-serene name of Murdering Sandhills. It was here, in 1868, that the brothers Lewis and John Pohlman stopped for dinner. Coming from Sydney, the Pohlmans were hawkers, travelling up the river with a dray and two horses, and selling their goods along the way. They'd had a good day of sales at Yanco Station, and planned to make Narrandera that night. However, their plans would change abruptly: the Pohlmans never left the sandhills.

A few days later, a Yanco stockman found the brothers' cart and horses and raised the alarm. Police discovered charred fragments of human bones nearby, as well as the Pohlmans' dog, its head smashed in. The hawkers' dinner camp had been fallen upon by three quite unpleasant characters known as Bob Campbell, Andy Digman and 'Big Jack': the trio had done them in, burned the bodies and rolled the dray off the road before fleeing into the bush. The profits of the slaughter were disappointingly thin: the Pohlmans had kept most of their cash in a hidden compartment in their wagon, and the murderers never found it: they had run off with a few mere trinkets. It's doubtful they considered, after the event, that it had been worth the effort.

Some eighteen months later, Campbell was caught. Digman, it's believed, was killed by his comrades soon after the murder of the Pohlmans. Where Big Jack got to, no one knows, though his lack of a real name must surely have aided him in evading identification. Campbell was hanged for the murders, saying before he died, 'One you've got, one you might get, one you will never get.' Which is terribly pithy but, if we're honest, very unhelpful.

So goes the story of how Murdering Sandhills got its name. But that quiet spot bears more than just a sinister name and a brutal history: like so many places where atrocities have been committed, something has been left behind to ensure the horror of the sandhills is never forgotten. Why this should be – why the commission of outrages in the material world causes the persistence of certain phenomena in the spirit realm – has never been satisfactorily explained, but no doubt it has something to do with murder victims tending to be a bit annoyed when they cross over to the other side, and the power of irritation to penetrate the boundary between the corporeal and the phantasmic, if you see what I mean.

It could be that the poor Pohlman brothers, who never completed their trip along the Murrumbidgee, are still, in death, trying to off-load their remaining merchandise. It could be that Bob Campbell and his dodgy mates have stayed behind at the sandhills to keep rummaging through the cart in search of a hidden fortune. It could be that the sandhills themselves are simply replaying their own memory of the nightmare that descended upon them that chilly autumn night.

Whatever the case, the fact is that many a drover who stops to rest by Murdering Sandhills has heard the creepy creak and the dreadful rattle of the Pohlman brothers' wagon as it rumbles on its way night after night. As the wheels bump and clack over the rough terrain, and the horses' hooves clip-clop with them, the blood of strong men freezes in their veins. For no dray passes by, no horses round the dunes. But the wagon, its cursed journey seemingly never complete, haunts the riverside and anyone unlucky enough to find themselves there.

It's not the ideal spot for a family camping holiday – unless your kids have been getting on your nerves lately and could do with a bit of a shock. But if you're out to be terrified, and to feel the dreadful tendrils of historic butchery reaching through the mists of time to coil themselves around your pounding heart – and be honest, you weirdos, there's more of you out there than you'd think – then Murdering Sandhills will do you just fine.

Albert

Hobart, Tasmania

In Salamanca Place stands Tasmania's Parliament House, a grand and imposing testament to the state's enduring conviction that it has enough people in it to need a parliament. It was built in the 1830s as the Customs House, but in the early 1900s, when Tasmania officially recognised that it had no customs to speak of, it became the dedicated seat of parliament.

Parliament houses tend to have lots of ghosts in them, but they are mostly of a minor and feeble type, haunting little nooks and crannies about the place, sitting in corners and bitching to themselves about preselections. It takes a special kind of ghost to stand out in a parliamentary environment, and Hobart has just such a ghost in Albert.

Albert Ogilvie was the twenty-eighth premier of Tasmania, a position he rose to after a successful legal career during which he became the youngest person in Australia to become a King's Counsel. Finding that his wig itched him terribly, he gave up lawyering and entered parliament, where he proved quite a bolshie little pinko: as premier, he abolished school fees, modernised hospitals, increased unemployment benefits and provided cheap housing loans to the poor, which was quite a coup given that, in the 1930s, poor people were generally considered to be nearly as unimportant as they are now.

So Albert did achieve quite a lot, and all by the age of forty-nine, when unfortunately he died in Victoria while playing golf, which did nothing for his image.* Incredibly irritated at being dead and therefore unable to complete his grand plan of turning Tasmania into a socialist paradise, Albert headed back to Hobart, settled in at Parliament House and resolved to spend the rest of his days – which theoretically could be infinite – making people jump and causing general feelings of unease.

Albert often likes to hang out around the Speaker's chair in the House of Assembly chamber, where he can look over the Speaker's shoulder and scoff at how ineptly they are keeping order in the House. It's said there's a disturbing icy presence in the chamber – many have reported a sudden feeling of deathly cold. Of course, this has to happen a fair few times before you cotton on to the fact that it's more than just the natural effects of being in Tasmania, but it's happened quite enough at Parliament House for MPs to determine that something funny is going on. It is old Albert, chilling the chamber with his spectral presence and intense annoyance at everything that's going on in his old workplace.

Former Speaker Sue Hickey claimed never to have met Albert, but said she welcomed any assistance he might want to give. 'If Albert could give me a few hints on how to keep the House ruly, I'd love to listen to them,' she said in 2019. Unfortunately, it's now believed that Hickey did not take Albert seriously at all, and that this was just an attempt at humour, something no decent politician should ever try. No wonder Albert hasn't made himself known to her: he had respect for the institution of government.

Often, late at night, Albert can be heard in the Parliamentary Library, looking through books and shuffling papers. Many times staff have heard the rustle of pages only to discover nobody there. It's Albert again – and there is something incredibly noble about a premier who died in 1939, yet to this day is invested enough in the responsibilities of his office and the welfare of his people that he will keep on reading up on developments in political science to make sure he's not falling

---

* Seriously, you'd be embarrassed, wouldn't you?

behind and is in a position to intelligently follow developments in state politics. Either that or he's reading books on the occult to find out how to bring himself back to life – and who could honestly say he wouldn't be welcome? Every state should have an Albert of its own.

The Stepmother from Hell

Fremantle, Western Australia

Even in the olden days, when hanging people was more a fun family day out than a law-enforcement technique, slipping the noose around a female neck was something not done lightly. To hang a woman was seen as somewhat unchivalrous, not really the done thing in polite society. So if a woman did find herself swinging, you can believe that the crime she was swinging for was a fairly heinous one.

So it was in the case of Martha Rendell, who met her end by the rope at Fremantle Prison on 6 October 1909. Several years previously, Martha had moved in with Thomas Morris, who was separated from his wife, and found happiness with her new man, albeit with one small reservation: his four children. At first she tried to deal with her feelings towards her stepkids in the traditional manner: by hitting them. She beat Thomas's daughter Annie so badly on one occasion that the girl couldn't walk.

Yet the beatings failed to satisfy Martha, who had a lifelong dream of not having to care for any children at all. She then had the bright idea of painting their throats with hydrochloric acid – nobody could ever call her unimaginative.

Witnesses said they had not only seen Martha Rendell administering the poison to the Morris children, but that she seemed to gain an unnerving amount of pleasure from causing them pain. One even claimed to have seen her masturbating while one of her victims screamed in agony; it's doubtful that this image did much to endear her to the jury.

After Annie (aged seven), Olive (five) and Arthur (fourteen) Morris had all died, ostensibly from diphtheria, Martha's attempts to polish off the last child, George, hit a snag when the boy fled the house and took refuge with his mother. After George accused his stepmother of trying to kill him, his siblings' bodies were exhumed for autopsy, and for Martha Rendell the game was up.

However, the preceding paragraphs need to be accompanied by a caveat, and that caveat is: unless she didn't. Because Martha went to the gallows proclaiming her innocence. The day before her execution, she made a statement which said, in part:

> I most solemnly wish to state that, on this last morning of my life, I am innocent of having done anything that injured the children in any degree. The spirits of salts were never used by me on the children. If I had done it I would confess. It would be contrary to my most solemn convictions to profess to man to be innocent when before God I should be found guilty, which to me would be dying with a lie on my lips and a crime on my soul unconfessed and unforgiven.

Now, take that with as many grains of salt as you like, but forensic science was not in those days what it is now,[*] and who can tell for sure whether the 'wicked stepmother', as the papers of the day dubbed her, really did put those three poor kiddies in their graves? And who can tell whether it isn't that burning sense of injustice that, even today, sees Martha Rendell gazing down upon the yard at Fremantle Prison?

Yes, there she is, as countless visitors to the prison – now a tourist attraction – have attested. When you look up at a certain high window, you will see her looking down, stony-faced, as if judging you for judging her. 'Who are you to condemn me,' she seems to ask, 'you who have

---

[*] They didn't even have *CSI*, let alone *CSI: Miami*.

never had to treat young children for diphtheria with limited medical expertise?'

Then again, perhaps the face in the window is begging for forgiveness. Perhaps, having failed to fess up in life, Martha Rendell is fated forever to stand at the window, staring out into infinity, hoping in vain that there will come someone to whom she can unburden herself of her sins and escape the prison her soul has been trapped in ever since her body was taken out of its own.

But that someone will never come, because the owners of the prison are making too much money from ghost tours, and they really need Martha to stay at the window. So at least someone has come out ahead as a result of three child murders. Silver lining.

The Headless Horseman
of Black Swamp

Black Swamp, New South Wales

In the wilds of south-western New South Wales, in the middle of the flat, marshy expanse known as the Black Swamp, on the road from Hay to Wanganella, a majestic sculpture stands proudly by the side of the Cobb Highway. In rustic red-brown iron, to match the hues of the outback, it depicts two drovers travelling down the track with a herd of cattle. But behind the drovers is another iron figure, a wild and dreadful one: the figure of the Headless Horseman. And he's chasing those drovers into infinity.

The Cobb Highway winds its way down through what was once called the Long Paddock: a tangled network of rough tracks connecting the rich markets of the south with the stock breeders of inland New South Wales. Thousands upon thousands of head of cattle would meander down along those tracks, passing through the Black Swamp on their way to sale. It was a dangerous path, and getting your herd through without encountering rustlers or bushrangers was a big ask. One drover, named Doyle, met his end in the Black Swamp at the hands of such a gang of brigands. But can a drover ever *really* die? Yes. He can. But Doyle's death was only the beginning of his story.

Throughout the 1860s and 1870s, drovers passing through the Black Swamp began to run into something even more terrifying than bushrangers.* When camping at night, they would hear the sound of soft hoofbeats approaching, presaging the arrival of a handsome grey cob,† trotting casually past and glowing faintly in the moonlight. On the horse's back sat a silent rider swathed in a long dark cloak, hat pulled down low. As he trotted by, sharp-eyed observers, straining their eyes in the gloom, would spot an unnerving detail: the horseman had no head. Or rather, he *had* one: it was just that he carried it under his arm.

Had 19th-century drovers had access to the World Wide Web, they would've been able to jump on *WebMD* and find out that, medically speaking, a head in the armpit is a bad sign. But even with their limited scientific knowledge, they knew that something was not right here, and they accordingly allowed the bejesus to be scared out of them without delay.

It became well known that the Black Swamp was not a place you wanted to camp in, for not only was the sight of the horseman on his cob trotting past your sleeping bag a petrifying one, there was a rumour that to see the Headless Horseman presaged your own imminent death. This rumour may indeed have been true: records indicate that none of the drovers who saw the horseman in the 1860s and '70s is alive today.

As is so often the case when spectres rear their spooky heads, there were those who sought personal gain from the phantom. A butcher from nearby Moulamein took to riding his own horse through drovers' camps, with his head hidden beneath his cloak, causing the cattle to stampede; he would then round up a few of the loose beasts to take back for himself. It just goes to show that as scared as we are of ghosts, they pale‡ into insignificance compared to the world's true scourge: butchers.

The actual Headless Horseman, on the other hand, seemed not to wish any harm to anyone, besides freezing their blood with terror. It was widely believed that the grey cob was simply taking Doyle on his last post-decapitation journey to the nether world, and the gibbering

---

* At least, until the bushranger shoots you, at which point the balance of terror shifts markedly.

† The horse, not the bread.

‡ Ha!

wrecks left in his wake were just unfortunate collateral damage. Others see his appearance as a warning to other drovers not to let Doyle's fate befall them.

It is a shame that Australia's homegrown Headless Horseman has never achieved the international fame of his American counterpart, but that's the power of Disney for you; if there's anyone who wants to plough some cash into a Black Swamp blockbuster, we await your call. For now, if you want to see a picture of the Riverina's very own Headless Horseman, check out the painting hanging in the bar of the Royal Mail Hotel at Booroorban. Or go take a look at that imposing roadside sculpture.

If you want to see the Headless Horseman himself, then simply pitch a tent in the Black Swamp and wait for nightfall, when you may well hear the sound of the grey cob's hooves clopping softly across the turf, and look up to see the space where a face ought to be.

The Spooks of Monte Cristo

Part One

Junee, New South Wales

Monte Cristo Homestead advertises itself as 'Australia's most haunted house', which in itself isn't all that impressive. I mean, anyone can advertise themselves as anything they want. This book, for example, is Australia's funniest ever book. See how easy it is?

But Monte Cristo has, if not an actual certificate proving its prime status, at least a few receipts backing its story up. It is an imposing old pile in Junee, in the Riverina region of New South Wales. Surrounded by gorgeous green scenery, the house is one of the loveliest examples of old-world charm to be found in Australia, and by day a delightful place to drop in for a Devonshire tea and a souvenir carriage wheel, if that's the sort of thing that gets your blood pumping.

If your arteries activate at more eldritch stimulants, however, you might rather visit Monte Cristo by night, where its popular ghost tours expose eager visitors to the full array of horrors that the homestead has to offer. The fact that the punters keep coming back suggests there is genuinely something eerie going on out Junee way. That or the place has some great booze.

Monte Cristo was built by local pioneer* Christopher William Crawley in 1885 on a hill overlooking Junee, so everyone in the town could look up every day and be reminded of how much richer he was

---

* An archaic word meaning 'white guy'.

49

than them. Crawley and his wife, Elizabeth, who found it so difficult to find a decent hobby that they had seven children, were happy at Monte Cristo, Elizabeth not even minding that her husband named their house after a depressing tale of obsessive revenge. But darker days lay ahead for the family, and the house.

In 1910, Christopher Crawley died at Monte Cristo of blood poisoning caused by a carbuncle on his neck that had become infected from rubbing against his starched collar. This was the kind of thing that happened all the time in 1910, what with the popularity of ludicrously high stiff collars combined with 'carbuncles' still being a thing. But Elizabeth never recovered from the shock of her husband's death, locking herself inside the house and shunning outside society in her grief. In the twenty-three years between Christopher's death and Elizabeth's, she only left the house twice, spending most of her time in a chapel she had built in the attic to make the house more like a horror-movie set. There she would stay, day after day, kneeling and praying and generally making herself as creepy as possible, so that when people told other people this story they'd feel cold and think they saw something fluttering out of the corner of their eye.

In 1933, Elizabeth Crawley died at the age of ninety-two of a ruptured appendix, but this was not enough to stop her. In fact, both of the Crawleys are said to be hanging around Monte Cristo, possibly because they get a cut of the ghost-tour takings. Christopher Crawley can be found haunting the room where he died, but despite his unfortunate and starchy demise, he is generally in a fairly genial mood, and those who wander into his territory need have no fear.

Elizabeth is a different matter. She was a difficult woman at the best of times, not that you could blame her: she had seven children, which would make anyone a little tetchy. But in death she has continued to exhibit the judgemental streak that her life as a compulsive breeder turned religious zealot had brought out in her. Anyone who enters her house can expect a quick summing up by the matriarch, and if she doesn't like you, she'll do her best to get you out of there.

Elizabeth Crawley's go-to move is the classic Invisible Freezer: she comes down on you in the form of a rush of ice-cold air that prickles on your skin and chills your bones as if you've been shut inside a meat locker, or just got an invitation to a fancy-dress party.* Sometimes she gets a little more specific, and you'll feel an actual hand on your shoulder, fingers digging into you as if to say, 'Did I spend twenty-three years praying in the attic like a loon just so the likes of *you* can come and eat scones in my living room?'

Mrs Crawley definitely doesn't take kindly to visitors, but her spiral into madness and subsequent incorporeal gatekeeping of her home was far from the end of Monte Cristo's nightmarish biography. But that's another chapter ...

---

*   Humanity's worst ever idea.

The Rage in Oakabella

Oakabella, Western Australia

In 2018, the new owners of Oakabella Homestead, thirty-five kilometres north of Geraldton in Western Australia, announced a major pivot in their marketing strategy. No longer would they promote Oakabella as a great place to see ghosts, because they'd found tourists were staying away from the place in fear of encountering one of the homestead's spirits. Put simply, Oakabella was just too scary to visit.

Nowadays, the owners try to entice you with a nice tea and a lesson on bush tucker, rather than inviting you to walk through the old house at night. But that doesn't mean the spirits have gone anywhere.

The doorways of Oakabella Homestead have bones built into them: the bones of black cats, which the builders put in to ward off evil energy. This might seem counterintuitive to some – one of the main requirements, you may think, of a non-evil house would be a total absence of cat bones in the doorframes. But different strokes for different folks. Whether the bones have worked is a matter of opinion: the energy in the house may not be evil, but neither does it seem particularly happy.

Oakabella was built in 1851 by wheat farmers keen to capitalise on the growing popularity of food among West Australians. From its earliest days, it seems to have been a place singularly plagued by bad luck. A three-year-old was crushed and killed when his bedroom window collapsed. A man was horrendously injured in an accident with dynamite, thus teaching him to stick with a rod and reel from then on. And then there was George.

George was an honest, hardworking fellow who wanted nothing more than a good job, a comfortable bed and a clean gun. It was the last of these that would prove his downfall, as when he was sitting on the aforesaid comfortable bed cleaning his gun, it suddenly fired, blowing George's unfortunate head clean off.

Ever since this tragic accident, George's room has been either a major attraction or a terrible repellent of Oakabella, depending on your perspective. George is not a happy ghost – not that you can blame him – and he will make his displeasure known to anyone who upsets him. One caretaker had her ankle broken in his room while trying to spruce the place up. On other occasions, efforts to rearrange George's furniture have resulted in a furious and prolonged banging noise until everything is returned to its original position.

George just doesn't like change: an attempt to paint the room pink resulted in the painter being yanked violently off her ladder. This was a man's room, George seemed to be asserting: none of this girly nonsense for me. It's this ghostly resistance to change that means the faint remnants of his blood can still be seen staining the walls.

It's not just George: those who've walked the halls at Oakabella have described feeling the dreadful weight of years of misfortune bearing down. There is a 'rage' in the homestead, they say – anger and frustration radiating from the sad souls within at their fates. Walking through the house, one can hear the faint creaking and knocking of restless spirits. In one room the smell of ashes fills the air, although no fire has been lit there for decades.

George's attitude to change seems to be shared by the inhabitants of the homestead in general. Vacuums break down when they're brought into the house, forcing staff to use brooms to clean up: they don't like anything new at Oakabella. And they're particular about who comes to call: most visitors have been welcome over the years, but others have set off some kind of spectral alarm system. One dodgy character was scared off when his entrance caused all the door handles in the house to rattle in unison until he vacated the premises.

Still, that's all behind us now, the new owners would like to assure you. Today you can come to Oakabella for a nice lunch and maybe a singalong round the campfire, with no need to worry about any ghosts. Of course, they can give no guarantee the ghosts won't worry about you.

Marybank's Heartbreak

Rostrevor, South Australia

The unfortunate fellow was simply a visitor to Marybank Estate, the stately home of Dora and Gerard Fox. Quite a cushy weekend he was in for, he'd wagered, for the Foxes' hospitality was renowned and Marybank well supplied with all the luxuries that the better class of person was accustomed to: good food and good wine, hot baths, fresh linen and so forth. Indeed, the chap's bed was a perfect delight: four posts, a splendid canopy and a mattress that embraced the sleeper like an old friend.

It was only very late in the night, perhaps midnight or even one o'clock, that the visitor discovered that his bedroom came with more accoutrements than he'd realised, and certainly more than he'd desired. For, woken by an ineffable sensation, he sat up and looked to the end of his bed – and what he saw ensured he slept no more that night.

It was a man, attired expensively but in a fashion suggestive of previous centuries. Atop his head was a powdered wig, and he struck a pose of a dandyish kind. Hardly the most horrifying sight one could see, except that the gentleman emitted an unnatural white glow, illuminating his immediate vicinity, and floated several inches above the ground. Looking towards the unhappy inhabitant of the bed, he nodded amiably, and then drifted straight through one of the bedposts, and then the bedroom door.

It was far from the only startling apparition to make its presence known at Marybank, a place with great sadness in its history. Gerard Fox was a descendant of Arthur Fox, the first of the family to own Marybank. He bought the place in 1853 and purchased the farm just three months later. Accidentally drowning in a shallow hole dug for sand by the River Torrens, Arthur left his widow and children to fight to keep control of Marybank and its intriguing collection of spirits.

Arthur's family would surely have been familiar with the nature of Marybank's phantasmic infestation. They would have heard the doors opening and closing in the night without human intervention. They may have heard the children playing hide-and-seek – so effectively, it would seem, that they were never found at all. Their affection for the house, however, was seemingly undimmed: perhaps they found it reassuring that Marybank was so well loved by the spirits that they insisted on remaining. Or perhaps they just foresaw what a lucrative sideline ghost tours would become in future years.

It was perhaps with that latter point in mind that Dora Fox, upon her death in 1995, decided to become a ghost – a career that obviously has many advantages. For it was after Dora passed away that a guest at the house spotted a distinguished woman in a long black dress drifting down the hall. That it was Dora is more than likely: it's entirely in keeping with her own sense of style that she would wear black, in mourning for herself.

Marybank Estate is above all a family home, and it seems that the ghosts who float about the manor are family-minded ones, many of them members of the Fox family hanging about to make sure their kin are keeping well. And yet the curious thing is that none of the ghosts have ever actually been *seen* by any of the Foxes. Heard, yes; seen, no. For some reason, the ghosts of Foxes prefer not to show themselves to their relatives, even while they keep a kindly eye on them.

You can see the ghosts, though, if you like. Marybank Estate is now known as Marybank Farm, and its website proudly proclaims it 'the perfect place for boutique weddings, garden elopements and secluded weekends away'. So if you want to see the lady in black or the gent in the powdered wig, or just hear the happy laughter of dead children, why not elope today?

The Asylum and the Music Box

Bundoora, Victoria

Abandoned asylums are such fertile ground for spirits that one might suspect that the mental healthcare sector of bygone eras was only set up to help develop new haunting talent. Of the numerous creepy old madhouses dotted around Australia, Larundel Asylum in Melbourne's northern suburbs is the equal of any in terms of shivers down the spine. It housed patients from the 1950s to the 1990s, but today the buildings of the old asylum, huddled around the central courtyard, are crumbling and ramshackle, heavily vandalised and graffitied.

The work of myriad young artists who have passed through the grounds since the asylum shut down, there's nothing particularly striking about the graffiti: just the usual mess of tags and scribbles. It's only in one spot that the artwork on the walls makes a visitor to the site stop dead in their tracks: in a bathroom filled with rubble, above a bath full of earth and debris, in huge red letters, are daubed the words 'HELP ME'.

Of course, it doesn't mean anything, nothing more than the odd bangs and crashes that can be heard coming from Larundel's dilapidated rooms and empty corridors. Falling masonry, most likely, or the scurrying of animals that have made their homes among the ruins. It means nothing. But there are other noises ...

The sounds of yelling voices ringing across the courtyard at night. Young children laughing. Babies crying. At least, so they say. Probably just the wind. But then … what about the music box?

On the third floor of Larundel Asylum, back before the buildings were condemned and the taggers and the possums moved in, there lived a girl. Just a tiny child she was, when she first arrived at the asylum – and it was no place for a tiny child. At least one serial killer was interned at Larundel, and countless other dangerous and violent patients passed through there to have their psychosis treated.

What the girl was in for is uncertain. The stories of her stay at the asylum don't include details of her malady, only of her loneliness and her poverty. For many years, that room on the third floor was her home, and her only possession a music box. Every day its melody would ring out on the third floor, as the little girl sat alone with only her tunes for company – unless you included the asylum staff, who were not known for either their compassion or their childlike whimsy.

The girl, as was traditional at old-time creepy asylums, died. We don't know how: could it have been a grotesque experiment gone wrong? Let's assume it was – it fits the mood better than, say, the flu. And convention has it that an unusual and grisly death is far more likely to turn a person into a ghost than a prosaic one. So it's safe to assume the poor little girl came to a nasty end, because from all reports she still hasn't budged from her room. At least, her music box hasn't.

Because people still, when they go to explore the unhappy wreckage of Larundel Asylum, report the strains of that music box tinkling down from the upper storeys. And they do not report finding it particularly comforting. On the list of 'things that if you hear them mean you are probably about to be attacked by a supernatural monster', eerie music boxes playing out of thin air rank pretty high, just below disembodied children's voices singing nursery rhymes and just above someone whispering 'get out of my house' in your ear.

One can easily imagine that the unhappy little girl keeps on winding her music box even in death because she's been robbed of her own voice and is using any means at her disposal to alert the living to her plight. One can equally easily imagine that the girl doesn't even know she's dead, and simply goes about her business in the fallen asylum, listening to her music box oblivious to the living world. One can easily imagine lots of things when you hear ghostly music in an abandoned mental hospital, even if you try really hard not to.

If you'd like to hear the ghostly music box of Larundel Asylum, you can find a short clip of it on YouTube. Just don't read the comments – they really spoil the mood.

The Cupboard in the Cop Shop

Deloraine, Tasmania

Down in the morgue at the old Deloraine Police Station, the white wooden door swings on its hinges, and the concrete slab lies cold and bare. Once, bodies lay on the slab, bodies that had attained their current condition in suspicious circumstances. Once, serious, straight-faced men poked and prodded at the corpses and tried to unlock the mysteries that the flesh hid. Concerned only with the bodies, if spirits rose from those carcasses and drifted through the bricks, they never noticed.

But some of the deceased did leave something behind, or at least that's the belief of the police officers who have passed through the Deloraine station. They say that the ghosts come from the morgue, souls departing their bodies but staying bound to the building.

One policeman tried to spend the night there, but found the task completely beyond him, as the spirits made their presence felt – and their presence was not conducive to a good night's sleep. As he laid down his head, a door creaked open somewhere in the station. A second later – *SLAM!* The officer sat bolt upright as the crash of it closing reverberated throughout the building. Out of bed he got, to do the rounds, check every corner of the station and make sure all was in order. There was nothing untoward. Nobody else was there, nothing

61

was out of place. He returned to his bunk.

As soon as he was horizontal: creak … *SLAM!* He barely caught himself before falling out of bed.

Around the station he went again, all alone, peeking into shadows and checking windows. As he walked, a freezing breeze suddenly swept through the corridor. A murmuring crept to the very edge of his hearing, indistinct voices, a faint buzzing in his head. He turned to return to the sleeping quarters, and the door right behind him banged like a gunshot.

Hurrying back to his room, he gathered up his things and left, swearing never to spend another minute in that place at night. The murmuring followed him out the door.

Slamming doors are common at Deloraine. One copper had to head to Westbury station to complete his work because the constant opening and closing of doors by no visible mechanism was making it impossible to concentrate.

But who is it playing silly buggers with the cops? Who's making it hard to work, and even harder to sleep, at Deloraine Police Station? Officer Delwyn Coad believes that the culprit is a friendly young woman who lives in a cupboard. One of the cupboards in the old police house at the station's rear, to be exact, which may explain why she feels a bit cramped when someone wants to sleep in there.

'For some reason, I think it's a she. I don't know why. I think because she's a gentle ghost, she's not violent, she's a friendly ghost,' said Coad, betraying her own internalisation of regressive gender roles. 'I think she comes in and out of the cupboard because the door keeps opening; you lock it and the next day it will be open.'

Certainly a lady ghost living in a cupboard is not the most frightening presence a police station could have in it – even most non-ghosts in the place are probably scarier. If the cupboard-dwelling spirit gets a little playful on occasion and gives officers the odd jump-scare, that is surely a small price to pay for having Tasmania's most interesting cop shop.

The Tale of Doctor Blood

Kapunda, South Australia

If you were writing a ghost story about the malevolent spirit of a mad doctor who in life performed unnatural experiments on human subjects, you would by no means name your central character 'Doctor Blood'. It would be laughably clichéd, a terribly amateurish, on-the-nose moniker that couldn't help but prevent any reader from taking your story seriously.

It's therefore incredibly irritating that when relating the tale of the sinister doctor of Kapunda, who performed experiments on human subjects and whose ghost now haunts the corridors of the North Kapunda Hotel, one runs up against the awkward yet irrefutable fact that his name was, in real life and honestly, no fooling, Doctor Blood.

To be precise, he was Dr Matthew Henry Smyth-Blood, but Dr Blood is how he liked to be known.* In fact, he changed his surname from the original Blood-Smyth to Smyth-Blood, placing the creepy bit last and declaring, 'I was born a Blood, and a Blood I will die!' As it happens, reports suggest he's stayed a Blood even longer than that.

Dr Blood was a distinguished gentleman who contemporary photographs show had a grim, sombre face and the kind of beard that would definitely arouse suspicion among decent people were it not for the fact that it was the 1800s and men were wearing all sorts

---

* Which you can't really blame him for.

63

of perverted facial hair. Blood was a popular doctor in the South Australian hamlet of Kapunda; he was also known as a keen amateur photographer[*] and prodigious snuff-taker.[†] He even rose to the station of Mayor of Kapunda, in which capacity he once entertained Prince Alfred, the Duke of Edinburgh, during his royal tour of 1867. Why Prince Alfred could be bothered travelling to Kapunda is a complete mystery: it'd be like if, today, Prince Harry decided to visit … well, Kapunda. But by all accounts the prince had a fine old time.

With all his renowned charm and years of public service, it's no surprise that Dr Blood's death was mourned by the whole town of Kapunda. He had died suddenly in his room, crying out in fear to his wife, Marianne, 'Mary, I cannot see you!' before expiring. His funeral procession was the longest seen in those parts for many years, testament to the good doctor's popularity.

Tales of his kindness and generosity were legion, but after his death other stories began to circulate. Stories of activities beyond the normal practice of a family doctor. Stories of medical perversions, of experiments being performed on humans that, to say the least, took a flexible approach to medical ethics. Dr Blood, it seems, had been living up to his surname in a far more direct manner than anyone had suspected. What he was actually trying to achieve with these experiments is uncertain. Searching for the secret to prolonging life? Stripping victims for parts in his efforts to reanimate dead flesh? Just cutting people up to create a spooky ambience? Anything is possible with a guy who deliberately calls himself Dr Blood.

And then the other rumours started spreading. Stories of how the doctor, perhaps touched by the outpouring of public affection following his demise, had decided to stick around. The North Kapunda Hotel was where he had welcomed the Duke of Edinburgh, the royal personage spending an afternoon at the old pub drinking and swapping stories with the locals. And it was apparently at the same hotel that Blood

---

[*] Red flag!

[†] RED FLAG!

decided to settle down, joining the other ghosts who make the North Kapunda Hotel, by some accounts, 'Australia's most haunted pub'.

The shade of Dr Blood stalks the hotel's rooms, quietly watching visitors and cursing the fact that he left his surgical instruments back in the land of the living. Stay the night there and you might be lucky enough to feel his cold presence creeping close behind you, or even catch a glimpse of that stern, unhappy visage, with its psychotic beard, staring out of an old mirror. If you wake up to the sensation of bony fingers lovingly exploring your vital organs ... check out early.

The House of Miracles

Guildford, New South Wales

Haunted houses are so often a downer, filled with screams and terror and ineffable sensations of impending doom. It's refreshing to find a feel-good haunted-house story: one which reaffirms your faith in the capacity of ghosts to make a positive contribution to society. Thus is the case with the Miracle House of Guildford, in Western Sydney.

As is generally the way with paranormal happenstance, the Miracle House's tale began in sadness, when seventeen-year-old Mike Tannous was tragically killed in a car accident in September 2006. Mike's family was, naturally, devastated, but forty days after he passed away, it seemed that Mike began to give his family some cause to hope that he did not die in vain. For it was then, just a few weeks after the tragedy, that the walls of the Tannous house began to produce oil.

Some called it a 'weeping wall', though it's debatable whether that term is appropriate for a wall that leaks oil. When a person weeps, after all, oil doesn't come out of their eyes – but maybe oil is to walls what saltwater is to people? Anyway, the oil began seeping from the wall, right above Mike's bed, and it just kept coming.

But it didn't just stay in that spot: before long, oil was streaming from beneath photos of Mike, religious iconography and walls all over the house. What's more, news spread: the Tannous family threw open their doors to pilgrims from all over the world who wished to witness the phenomenon for themselves. And while 'travelling overseas to see some oil running down a wall' doesn't instantly sound like the most exciting trip a person could possibly take, it has to be conceded that oil appearing spontaneously on a wall is one of the most interesting kinds of oil there is. It's a lot more interesting, for example, than that which has simply been poured on a wall.

But the thing about Mike Tannous's post-mortem oil is that it did a lot more than simply ooze down walls like the moody goo from *Ghostbusters II*.* This is some seriously helpful oil.

One woman came to the Miracle House having been told by doctors that she would never be able to fall pregnant. Having exhausted her medical options, she thought, 'Why not give ol' Mike a try?' And so she came to the Tannouses', bowed before the wall and prayed. One month later she returned to the house with a box of chocolates. She was pregnant! Mike had done the trick. And though he couldn't really eat the chocolates, he appreciated the gesture. It was clear that while other spirits might hang around after death harassing the living, scaring the living daylights out of them or just sort of mournfully moping about the place, Mike Tannous had decided to be the change he wanted to see in the world.

There have been other reports of miracles being done by the spirit of Mike Tannous. The family claims he even cured cancer on one occasion. Clearly, the late teenager is following in the proud tradition of ghost doctors, the most famous of which in this country is of course Mary MacKillop. MacKillop is currently Australia's only saint, while Mike has yet to be canonised. Is this due to reverse sexism at the Vatican? Who knows? (Yes.)

Besides the scandalous snubbing of Australia's greatest ghost doctor of the 21st century, though, the big question remaining is: why oil? Some, of course, scoff at the idea that a spirit who has passed on to the next world would manifest itself in the form of an oily wall; but it seems no more absurd than the many other ways in which phantasms come to

---

* Underrated movie, just quietly.

us. Who made the rule that pushing furniture around was some kind of authentic haunting? If the Tannouses' walls were dripping blood, everyone would agree that it was classic ghost behaviour – but because it's oil we're supposed to disregard it?

Fortunately, this is no historical haunting: the House of Miracles is there right now, welcoming anyone who wants to partake of the comfort of Mike's oil. If you want to see for yourself the miracle, and judge for yourself whether it's the kindly spirit reaching out or just a bunch of oil, head down and give it a squiz.

Ghosts of Murray Park

Campbelltown, South Australia

At Campbelltown Library in Adelaide can be found the Links Wall Hanging, a huge hand-sewn piece of fabric depicting the geography and history of the City of Campbelltown. Named 'Links' because it links the past to the present, and 'wall hanging' because it is hanging on a wall, the piece has many fascinating details, such as Violet Farm, Rob Smith's hot air balloon and the Anzac Monument. But the most fascinating detail of all can be found in the depiction of a large, slightly gingerbready house, partially obscured by trees, next to St George's Church and just in front of the Vine Street Rose Garden. A close look will reveal that, in the first-floor bay window, a dark figure is standing looking out.

For this is Murray House, previously known as Murray Park, and whoever sewed that particular square on the wall hanging knew that on the first floor of Murray House, a ghost is walking.

Murray House was built in 1881 for Alexander Borthwick Murray, and extended in 1910 by his son, South Australian chief justice Sir George Murray. Today it stands on the grounds of the University of South Australia's Magill Campus, a terrible fate for any historic building as it means that inevitably students are going to get in. And when they do, they are likely to be working on various projects in there, like immersive theatre.

It was during just such a performance that student Glenn Rafferty met May. May appears to be a young girl of around that age when girls begin to be interested in terrible singing groups. She is well past that, though, having died long before even the Bay City Rollers were conceived of. According to Glenn Rafferty, May dressed in a manner akin to a character in *Picnic at Hanging Rock* – and we can't rule out the possibility that she actually is one of the girls who disappeared at Hanging Rock. After all, we never did see where they went: it's entirely possible they ended up at UniSA. Or *would* be entirely possible if it weren't for the fact that *Picnic at Hanging Rock* is entirely fictional. Then again, many people believe that it's based on a true story – and in a democracy, who are we to deny them their opinion?

The point is that, while standing at the entrance hall to Murray House, waiting for his theatrical performance to begin, Mr Rafferty saw May – twelve or thirteen years old, with long golden hair – standing on the landing at the top of the stairs, looking at him curiously. He thought little of it, assuming, as many of us do when seeing a little girl, that he had simply seen a little girl. It was only when May appeared to him again the following night, with a look of excitement on her face at seeing him, and then proceeded to walk straight through the wall, that Glenn Rafferty began to smell a phantom.[*]

May could be the girl who others have claimed to see on the stairs, believed to be the daughter of a maid who once worked at Murray House. Or there may be two young girls living in Murray House – or not living in Murray House, as it were. There is certainly at least one adult ghost there as well, and it is this woman who is apparently the figure seen in the bay window.

She is a young lady, attired in the fashion of around the time of Murray Park's construction, and she walks along the first-floor balcony, over and over again – except for when she is standing at that bay

---

[*]   Glenn's story, by the way, can be heard in a YouTube video titled 'The Haunting of Murray House', which also features gripping scenes such as a noise that could possibly be a man saying 'hello' and a psychic who points at doors.

window, looking out, beckoning to people on the street to come inside. We shouldn't automatically assume that the reason she wants them to come inside is a horrible one, but there's a fair chance it is. Especially if you're a student.

The Restless House at Lane Cove

Lane Cove, New South Wales

The house was old. A hundred and ten years old it was, when the McDougall brothers were living there. An ordinary house it was, in Lane Cove, but even the most ordinary house, if it stands long enough, amasses stories, and stories have a habit of hanging about, whether they're wanted or not.

This house had a story from its earliest days, way back in the middle of the 19th century. The owners back then, it was said, had a little girl who met a terrible end. Fell down a well in the yard, so it was said. Never seen again. Not seen. But … not gone, either. The poor little thing never really left, maybe. Perhaps she was trying to get out, or to send a message. Maybe she just wanted to play.

Mr McDougall, who owned it in the 1950s, was sitting by the fire of an evening, reading, starting to doze. His brother likewise, in the other chair, feeling his eyelids grow heavy as the night closed in and bedtime beckoned. It was as still and peaceful a scene as could be imagined. Until …

There was a clinking and a clanking, out of nowhere. Soft at first, then quite insistent, as if someone was trying to get the men's attention. It shattered the serenity of the winter night, and shook the brothers from their torpor. Mr McDougall blinked and spluttered. His brother started from his chair.

The fire irons, hanging from the mantel, were swinging and shaking and clanging against each other. The clinking and clanking continued, like a kitchen cupboard in an earthquake, as the irons swayed to and fro in the wind. The only oddity was that there *was* no wind. The irons were swaying, it seemed, entirely of their own accord.

Mr McDougall's brother, a man of infinite practicality, set to discovering the source of the surprising cacophony. 'A draught,' he nodded sagely, and walked to the door to ensure it was closed securely against outside chills. It was. No breath of air was infiltrating the room: certainly none of sufficient violence to set the irons swinging as they were.

'Ah!' said Mr McDougall's brother, finally hitting upon what he was sure was the solution. 'There is a floorboard loose,' he explained to Mr McDougall. 'When the floorboard moves, it sets the irons to swaying.' He dropped to his knees and began investigating the floor. The embers in the fireplace burned low as he shuffled across the floor, checking the boards one by one. Finally, he rocked back on his haunches and chewed his lip. In his chair, Mr McDougall scratched his head. The fire irons just kept swaying and banging against each other, and the air around them continued to be as stubbornly still and placid as ever.

From then on the brothers were in no doubt whatsoever that they had a guest in the house. Were the movement of objects about the house under the propulsion of no detectable force not enough, there was the fact of dinner. For every night, at dinnertime, Mr McDougall's brother would set the table. Two places, for two brothers.

Except that it was never just two places. It was three. Even if they had guests, there would always be an extra place. Mr McDougall's brother could not explain how it was that every single night he laid an extra place at the table, and yet he could not deny that he was doing it. There was no way around it: something far stronger than his own will had decreed that there would be an extra guest for dinner, and he was powerless to refuse it.

The McDougalls never came to any harm at the hands of the spirit who shared their house. Indeed, after the initial understandably unnerving period, they settled down to a peaceful life with their housemate, and learned to tolerate the odd dropped glass or rattled window. For how could two such kind and generous gentlemen object to showing indulgence towards a lonely little girl, who so long ago had met tragedy a bare few yards from where they sat, the night the irons set to swinging?

Terror of Tailem Town

Tailem Bend, South Australia

Looking for a holiday experience that combines valuable education about Australian history with the thrill of seeing mannequins in period costume? Are you interested in learning about how people sent mail in the olden days or how they saddled a horse? Do you want to see a police car with bullet holes, several different kinds of barbed wire and an eccentric owner? Would you like to be stalked and manhandled by numerous ghosts and feel yourself possessed by a sudden, inexplicable rage?

If you answered yes to all these – and, heck, why wouldn't you? – then you want to head down the Princes Highway, an hour or so east of Adelaide, to the banks of the Murray River and the Old Tailem Town Pioneer Village.

It's a place where history comes alive, and you get to experience what it would have been like to live in an affordable rural tourist attraction. Colonial-era buildings, sourced from all around the country, jostle up against each other in an authentically ramshackle little hamlet. There's also an array of old cars, buggies and train carriages in varying states of rust, so people can also get a sense of what it was really like to visit an old scrapyard.

The fact that Old Tailem Town was constructed Frankenstein-style, from historic buildings from elsewhere, means that it occupies a unique place among ghostly locations. Rather than being haunted by those who died on the spot, spirits have been trucked in from myriad other spots to rub shoulders in the pioneer village.

The disappointing thing about ghosts, of course, is that even though they frequently spring up in places of historical interest, where visitors come to learn more about their country's past, they hardly ever make use of their expertise to educate the public. The spirits of people who actually lived in colonial times could be employed to great effect in Old Tailem Town, giving eyewitness accounts of horseshoe-making and dysentery. But sadly, the ghosts of Tailem, like those everywhere, it seems, are more interested in sinister lurking than enlightenment.

What you feel in Old Tailem Town could disturb you more than what you see. Some have reported entering the village and feeling something start to choke them. Others have said that after spending some time in Old Tailem, they're overwhelmed by anger and hatred, and a desire to lash out at those around them. Certainly there is tragedy in the tales of some of the places around the town – terrible accidents and murders among them. In one of the houses, children are believed to have died. The powerful emotional jolt that the town inflicts on visitors may well be an expression of the collective unhappiness stored in the former dwellings and stores.

And there *is* a bit to see as well. The old church seems to be the centre of town, apparition-wise. A man's ghost loiters in the shadows at the back of the chapel, watching visitors. He has been distinctly identified by numerous witnesses, but if any light is turned on him, he vanishes. He could be seen as a protector of the church, watching to make sure nobody does any damage. But that might just be putting a positive spin on things. The chances that he's a malevolent spirit lying in wait for prey are just as good, really.

The ghosts of Old Tailem Town mainly seem to simply want company. Walking through town, it's common for tourists to be pursued by footsteps, voices and whistling, as if the bored spirits just want to join in with the touring parties. But then again, there is that anger that comes upon a person … Maybe what the Tailem community wants most of all is some solid bodies to take control of, and then … Best not to think about it.

Whepstead Manor

Wellington Point, Queensland

According to the website Funzug.com,* Whepstead Manor, at Wellington Point, Queensland, is the second-scariest house on Earth, behind only the Amityville Horror house in the US, where a number of horrific murders took place in the 1970s, causing the property to be plagued by ever more horrifying attempts at a film franchise.

Now, this book has no way of verifying the qualifications of the team at *Funzug*, so it would be reckless to consider that rating as being in any way official. But neither can we simply dismiss the *Funzug* scale: Whepstead may not be the second-scariest house on Earth, but if the 'zug says it is, it's got to be at least top twenty.

Whepstead Manor was built in 1889 for Gilbert Burnett, a fabulously wealthy landowner who had made it big in the sugar mill business, before moving on to make it even bigger in the sawmill business. He may have gone on to succeed with ever more fascinating kinds of mills had he not gone bust in 1891, forcing him out of the magnificent villa he had built at Wellington Point.

The grand white house, which stands at the end of a wide, tree-lined drive amid scenic greenery, went through a succession of owners before becoming the Bay View Private Hospital in 1943. In 1973, it went back

---

* 'Where Fun Never Ends', apparently.

to being just a house, and since then has done time as a restaurant and function centre. Perhaps you could hire it for your next party … IF YOU DARE!*

To spend any amount of time at Whepstead Manor is to have your nerves tested to their very limit. It'll start subtly: at first you may notice nothing untoward at all. And then … the faint whiff of lavender in the air, gradually growing stronger. The source of the scent: undetectable. For this is the perfume of Martha Ann Burnett, Gilbert's wife, the first lady of the house.

Then you may notice certain oddities. Lights flickering on and off. Objects moving around. Stains appearing on walls and carpets, out of nowhere. You might see a face in a mirror, just for an instant, gone as quickly as it appeared. Maybe it was that of Martha Ann, or one of her children.

It's said that one of the Burnetts' daughters vanished without trace. Some say she fell to her death from a window; others that she disappeared while out for a walk and was never seen again. You might see her walking from room to room at the manor, or hear her running along the corridors. At night you may hear her softly crying, somewhere.

Or you might see her brother. The little boy was rumoured to be a cripple, with a withered leg. His face has been seen peeping through the railings of the central staircase, though he's never on the stairs when you walk up them. The lonely boy watches you, but melts away if you try to find him.

What with the inexplicable scents, the malfunctioning lights, the moving objects, the creepy faces in the mirrors and the terrifying little kids scuttling about the place, it seems odd that anyone would want to do anything but get the hell out of there within an hour of arriving. But for those who summon up their courage, there is more to come. Walk through the rooms of the mansion and you might have the privilege of feeling a sharp tug on your hair. You can probably guess that if you feel

---

* (Crashing chord …)

that tug and turn around to see who it was, there'll be no one there.

They say the matron of the old Bay View Private Hospital used to grab hold of her underlings' hair to get their attention. It seems likely that the method is still effective on visitors to the manor today.

Keep your courage up and you may make it upstairs to the attic, where you will find the butler. Or, at least, an old man in a butler's uniform and a bowler hat. This man, too, can be seen in the mirrors around the house. He doesn't do much: possibly in his living days he served the family well and faithfully, but these days his only job seems to be to creep you the hell out. Which does seem to be the Burnett family's main occupation too, so he's still serving them well and faithfully.

Second-scariest house on Earth? Maybe, maybe not, but it sure is an exhausting day out.

Cell 17

Melbourne, Victoria

Ghosts love to hang around prisons. Or, rather, they probably hate hanging around prisons but they have no choice, as whatever chains bind a spirit to the earthly realm seem particularly strong in places of correction. It's no surprise that prisons are fertile grounds for phantasmic activity, as the souls that depart their bodies in such places are apt to have been in a state of some agitation at the moment of demise. Ned Kelly, for example, was said to be extremely distressed shortly before his execution, which many historians attribute to the fact that he was about to be executed.

Kelly's ghost, however, has been conspicuous by its absence since his death, and it's generally assumed that, whatever his feelings about the hanging, his spirit found peace with the knowledge of the incredible merchandising opportunities that it created. At the site of his end, however, there are plenty of restless souls willing and able to drum up some publicity for the tourist trade.

For that trade is the only business being done nowadays at Old Melbourne Gaol, the forbidding pile of stone and steel on Russell Street, which from 1845 to 1924 took in the most notorious of Victoria's ne'er-do-wells and today allows paying customers to get a taste of what it was like to be a victim of the brutality of the prison–industrial complex. Visitors may enter the tiny cells that once held murderers, rapists, thieves and jaywalkers, and even stand upon the gallows that dealt out old-timey justice.

There are many reports of supernatural occurrences at Old Melbourne Gaol: more than one tourist has told of seeing a looming figure in the doorway of a cell. Some tales are more embellished, including details like flesh rotting off the bones of these figures. But one cell in particular, it is agreed, is the most haunted of all within the prison grounds: Cell 17.

It's not known exactly who dwells in Cell 17 nowadays: no doubt a motley procession of fiends and blackguards spent their time huddled in there over the years. Nor is it known why the current occupant seems so angry.

No person, corporeal or not, can be seen by the latter-day guests of Cell 17, but someone certainly makes his presence felt to those who invade his personal space. For if you dare to cross the threshold of that particular cell, you may well be letting yourself in for a spectral pummelling.

In Cell 17 people have been pushed, thrown against the wall, punched and slapped. They have come out of the cell sporting scratches that weren't there before, as the spirit within kicks and claws and flails with all its might to send the message that the living are not welcome. Ironically, this only makes the cell more popular with visitors: if only ghosts were better able to understand unintended consequences and the principles of marketing. Then again, maybe it can and it's doing it all deliberately to draw more punters in: providing a bespoke service to those who enjoy getting beaten up by invisible convicts.

If that's you, then Cell 17 is where you should head without delay. If you're not so masochistic, but still curious, then do pop your head around the door – but be prepared to beat a hasty retreat once things start getting rough. If, on the other hand, you are squeamish or of a delicate constitution, it may be best to stick to the surrounding cells, where you might experience an eerie atmosphere and even catch a glimpse of something sinister: but at least you won't actually get yourself belted up by a spook with a chip on its shoulder.*

---

* Of course, invisible spectres don't really have shoulders, but prominent parapsychologists believe they are still capable of having chips on them. Besides which, the ghost in Cell 17 must have some kind of shoulder to be able to throw punches like he does.

The Hectorville Spectres

Hectorville, South Australia

The oldest house in Hectorville has a history that could accurately be described as 'unfortunate'. It was built in 1849 in Binnswood Street, next to Fourth Creek, for the pastoralist Price Maurice, a man who never recovered from the trauma of his first and last names being the wrong way round. After a while, he had to return to England to regain his health, as living at Fourth Creek – whether it be rising damp or an allergy to his sheep – had made him thoroughly sick.

In August 1864, the Hawkins family arrived in Hectorville and in September they purchased the house, renaming it 'Cosford' after their house in England, as to have more than one house name in one's lifetime was considered dreadfully vulgar.

Just a month after moving in, Mrs Anna Hawkins was thrown from her horse, which then kicked her, with fatal results. The *Adelaide Express* demanded an enquiry into how 'so savage a brute' as this horse could've been 'sold as fit for a lady to ride': an editorial view which failed to take into account a) what massive jerks humans usually are to animals, and b) the plain bad luck with which the Hawkins family was cursed.

For it was less than two years after Anna Hawkins died under the hoof that her husband passed away too – in far less violent circumstances – leaving their four daughters and two sons parentless. The house was then leased to Alfred Ward in December 1866. Later that month his wife died. In February 1867, their fifteen-year-old daughter passed away.

By that time, the message seemed clear: anyone who moved into this house was dicing with death in a very real way. And yet people kept living there, in spite of everything – which just goes to show that if a property is big and fancy enough, there will always be someone willing to live in it, no matter how likely it is to kill them.

Later on, as successive owners realised that the house at Hectorville was clearly swarming with ghosts, they shrugged it off with the conviction that the spectres were 'friendly'. Which may well have been true, but few seem to have considered the likelihood that the ghosts, being indeed friendly, were desperately trying to warn people to get out before it was too late.

For example, one night Mr James Moran, who dwelled at Cosford in the early 21st century, was awakened by the terrible crash of a cupboard, previously bolted to the wall, falling to the ground. 'There is no way it could have fallen off by itself,' he said. 'It had help.' But he still didn't get the hint, despite noting that the whole house frequently smelled of 'snuffed-out candles'. Which is a pungent metaphor if ever I sniffed one.

But Moran did sell in the end, as they all do. For they grow weary of the voices, and the footsteps upstairs. They grow tired of the chilling presence in the mansion's twelve rooms and the claustrophobic sense that they are sharing the house with dozens of invisible others. They grow sick of the falling furniture and the bizarre odours and the melancholic ambience of a place where death once seemed to pursue with relentless determination anyone with the temerity to live in it.

Still, if you don't mind the presence of restless spirits who you can convince yourself with enough positive self-talk are 'friendly', you might want to make an offer on Cosford yourself. It's an imposing estate, and will probably set you back a couple of million dollars, but if you can stir up the ghosts a bit, you never know: the price might get slashed. And, as they say, a haunted bargain is still a bargain.

Quinn's Light

Springfield, New South Wales

Quinn's Light, it was called, for it was John Quinn who first saw it. From his homestead at Springfield, a sprawling sheep property in the Dudauman Valley, he spotted it, glowing golden in the night sky, drifting down from the top of Gogobilly Hill.

Now, John Quinn was no mad dreamer or rambling drunk. He was known neither for his wild stories nor for his inability to distinguish reality from fantasy. He was widely respected in the area for his good sense and skill with dogs. With his kelpie Wallace, he had won the first Federal Sheepdog Trial in 1901, and would go on to become perhaps Australia's most respected sheepdog-trial judge. All in all, the gentle giant was as sober and rational a fellow as ever stood looking out over his paddocks at sundown, stroking his beard and nodding with quiet wisdom. It was while he was doing just that, in fact, that he saw the light.

It was bright, so bright as to be almost blinding when John looked directly at it, and it appeared to be shaped vaguely like an eagle or some other great bird of prey, floating down the valley with outstretched wings. Like an angelic vision from the Good Book, it shone with a fierce gold aura, lighting up the trees below as it came slowly across the woods and fields. Passing over Springfield, as John Quinn stared in wonder and fear, the apparition circled the homestead and returned whence it came, gliding back to the west until it faded and vanished among the hills.

John Quinn was a sensible man. He did not assume that just because he had seen a huge golden heavenly eagle circling his farm, there must necessarily *be* a huge golden heavenly eagle circling his farm. The eyes and the brain can trick a man, after all. He was willing to write this occasion off as one of those tricks, or even a dream. When the light appeared to him several more times, however, he recognised that he had some hard thinking to do. Either he was being visited in the evenings by an unnerving, if beautiful, other-worldly presence, or he was out of his tiny little mind. It was important to John that he find out which it was.

Accordingly, he went to his friends and asked them to come to Springfield and have a look at the light for themselves. As night came down on the valley, John Quinn held his breath, and then let it out in a sigh of relief when he heard his friends gasp and exclaim: they too saw the light, and goggled in wonder as it floated towards them and did its circuit of the homestead.

The reality of Quinn's Light had been established to the satisfaction of all. But what *was* it? Being a practical man of the outback, Quinn decided to take the only course of action that a practical man of the outback could. Turning to his pals, he muttered, 'Let's go get it.'

And so began the ride of Quinn's Posse.

The next night, a team of riders set out from the Springfield homestead, intent on chasing down and capturing the great golden luminescence. As the eagle shape once again rounded the house and set off for its home in the hills, the men spurred their horses after it. But though the horses galloped with all their might and the riders tracked the light all the way to Gogobilly Hill, and though the light seemed to drift slowly through the night sky, there was no catching it. As the party struggled up the slopes, it simply vanished, and they were left in the dark, with nothing to do but turn for home.

And so Quinn went to Plan B: shoot it. Gathering the district's sharpest-eyed hunters, he dispatched them to bring the light down with rifles. As it came down the valley, they fired straight and true – but to the surprise of, well, basically no one, bullets seemed to have no effect on the mysterious glow in the sky. Even John Quinn had to admit it had been a supremely optimistic scheme.

To this day, the source and nature of Quinn's Light remains a mystery. John Quinn himself carried on with his life, breeding his kelpies, judging his dog trials and being respected and distinguished in a variety of locations. But never did he discover the truth behind the spectacular light in the valley, why it came to him or where it went when it faded away for good.

The Digging Man

Canberra, Australian Capital Territory

Canberra's Government House, commonly dubbed Yarralumla, is a gorgeous old mansion on the banks of Lake Burley Griffin, set amid 130 acres of lush parkland once occupied by a thriving sheep station. Built on the remains of the 1830s homestead first established by Francis Mowatt, the property's most constitutionally significant occupant today is the Governor-General of Australia, for whom Yarralumla is an important home base for doing whatever it is he does.*

The most interesting resident of Yarralumla, however, is not the vice-regal personage but one who has been on the grounds for far longer. In fact, he's been there longer than the nation of Australia itself, having been wandering the acreage since the days when Yarralumla was a sheep station and the countryside infested with bushrangers.

The story, you see, goes like this. In 1826, one James Cobbity was robbed on a cattle station in Queensland by a convict, who relieved him of a large diamond. The convict was later caught, but the gem was never recovered. The thief, in fact, had given a friend a map, which led him to the spot where the diamond had been hidden. That friend then found it and kept it until he died, whereupon his son started out from his southern New South Wales home for Sydney, to sell the gem, in the company of his servant, a young Aboriginal man.

---

* I think it's mostly holding morning teas.

Between Cooma and Queanbeyan, the son and his companion were set upon by bushrangers. The servant was shot dead, the bushrangers burying him under a nearby deodar tree – which makes them pretty well mannered, as bushrangers go: most members of that profession were very much of the 'leave you to the buzzards' school of etiquette.

The bushrangers, though, for all their respect for the dead, were not rewarded with the diamond – it was never found. There was a good reason for this: the servant, before being gunned down, had taken the precaution of swallowing the jewel for safekeeping. A measure the utility of which was much reduced by his death and interment, of course, but you can see how it might've seemed a good idea at the time.

But the story doesn't end there.* For the spot where the two travellers were ambushed, and where the unfortunate diamond swallower was buried, was no random patch of countryside. In fact, they were on the grounds of the Yarralumla sheep station, then owned by a Colonel Gibbes. And although it was then simply a sprawling sheep run, the relentless march of progress and the advent of Federation meant that in 1913 it became the site of Government House, the new residence of the Governor-General of Australia.

But though the homestead became grander and the grounds more sculpted, that old deodar tree stayed put, and so did the Aboriginal man who had been laid beneath it, but who had not rested in peace. For residents and visitors to Yarralumla over the years have reported the same thing: a tall, thin, lonely figure walking the grounds, restless and questing. He stalks the parklands at night with an eerie glow, and can be seen most often by the deodar tree, where he falls to his knees and appears to dig frantically, trying to break through the solid earth to recover the diamond that he took to his grave.

An unsigned letter, dated 1881, passed to the Commonwealth by the property's former owners, testifies to the presence of the Digging Man many years before Yarralumla came into vice-regal possession. Indeed,

---

* I mean, really, you're far enough into this book by now to know that the story never ends there.

since the 1840s he would appear to have been roaming the acreage in search of the precious cargo that was entrusted to him.

Whether it's a sense of duty that compels him to try to complete the journey he set out on all those years ago, or just a desire to profit from his knowledge of the treasure's hiding place, it would seem he has been doomed to failure. For no matter how many times he kneels beneath the deodar, and no matter how long he digs in the moonlight, ghostly hands cannot penetrate real soil. The poor man must simply dig … forever.

The Grouchy Major

Albany, Western Australia

Patrick Taylor Cottage is a creepy place. Not creepy in a Gothic castle way, or even in a ramshackle old cottage with creaky floorboards way. In fact, from the outside Patrick Taylor Cottage is the sweetest little house imaginable. Neat and clean, with charming stone chimneys and a vibrant and well-kept garden, it's every bit the kind of lovely little village dwelling you imagine the kids from the Faraway Tree books living in.[*] It's a credit to the current owners, who have kept it in splendid condition, for Patrick Taylor Cottage is the oldest surviving residence in Western Australia, built in 1832. As such, it's taken a lot of work to maintain its pristine facade.

Inside the cottage is a series of beautifully preserved tableaux of colonial Australian domesticity. Crammed full of charming old furniture, china tea sets and the odd spinning wheel, it's the perfect place to go to get a sense of history while trying very hard not to knock anything over.

Sadly, though, the current management has opted to make it creepy. This has been done via the somewhat overused – in historical re-creation circles, anyway – technique known in the trade as 'filling your house with unsettling dolls'. They're everywhere in the old house:

---

[*] Which, admittedly, could be considered creepy in itself, when you consider what those kids got up to.

at the piano, at the spinning wheel, cooking breakfast in the kitchen. It mightn't be so bad if it were just the little rag dolls and porcelain dolls scattered about the place, as if it were the domain of a horrendously spoiled yet old-fashioned child.

But what really gives the casual visitor to Patrick Taylor Cottage the screaming heebies is that many of the dolls are life-size. And they stare at you with their lifeless eyes, as if to say, 'As soon as your back is turned, we are going to jump you and sink our mannequin fangs into your tender flesh like those statues from *Doctor Who*.'*

It is incredibly disturbing to walk into a tourist attraction and come face to face with an immobile young woman sitting on the bed. Because your brain's first reaction is that it's *someone*. It makes one wonder how many ghost sightings throughout history have been caused by overzealous tourism operators.

There is one ghost, however, at Patrick Taylor Cottage who is clearly more than just an ill-judged dummy – at least, not in the inanimate object sense. This is a bad-tempered fellow whose eccentric habits leave no one in any doubt that he is the real deal.

Major Frederick Ingoldby was a bluff, irascible old Yorkshireman who retired to Albany after a distinguished medical and military career. He had served in the Boer War as a surgeon major, sawing off limbs and such with great skill and care. After the war he attempted to retire to England, but upon being reminded that the weather sucked, and longing for the sunny climes he remembered from the war, he opted instead to live out his remaining years in a place climatically almost identical to South Africa but 5 to 10 per cent less racist: Western Australia.

He moved into Patrick Taylor Cottage, which was as quintessentially English a corner of the wide brown land as one could hope to find, and pottered away happily for the rest of his life in the company of his dear wife, Annie, reflecting on his accomplishments and telling kids to get off his lawn. But he always did have a short temper and when he died

---

* If you don't get this reference, go look it up – it's awesome.

on 15 September 1940, aged eighty-one, it left him incredibly irritated. Fortunately, whatever authority is in charge of such things was able to provide him with an outlet for his rage.

This is why, every year, on the anniversary of his death, Major Ingoldby returns to Patrick Taylor Cottage and kicks up one hell of a fuss. Like a phantasmic version of the sea captain's cannon in *Mary Poppins*, he barges his insubstantial way into the building and starts throwing his weight around. Furniture gets moved, display cases holding semi-fascinating historic relics get pushed over, and those china tea sets start flying through the air. Visitors to the house on 15 September would be well advised to keep both eyes open, lest they find a spinning wheel hurtling at their heads.

And yet the owners and staff of Patrick Taylor Cottage are happy to have the major there, because although he's a terrible grump and has very little respect for the fixtures, he has personality. Which is more than you can say for the possibly satanic mannequins standing around the place. And if you want to attract people to an old house, a ghost with charisma makes all the difference.

The Spooks of Monte Cristo

Part Two

Junee, New South Wales

We've already covered the matter of Christopher Crawley, the builder of Monte Cristo Homestead, and his unhappy wife, Elizabeth, who creeps around the corridors giving chills to paying guests. But a place doesn't earn the sobriquet 'Australia's most haunted house' just because of one creepy couple. This old farmhouse has seen a lot more tragedy in its time, and is currently positively crawling with unhappy paranormals who can't find their way to the afterlife.

If you go to Monte Cristo today – and it'll only cost you fifteen bucks to do so, or $125 if you want dinner, or $195 if (god help you) you want to stay the night* – you will find on one of the stairs leading up to the front door a patch of concrete that doesn't match the rest of the staircase. It's discoloured, a lighter shade than the surrounding steps. And it might stun you to learn this, but the reason it's a lighter shade than the others is – brace yourself – a *spine-chilling one*.

For it seems that the Crawleys had a maid. And it seems that this maid was a very good maid. So good, in fact, that Mr Crawley engaged her for certain *extra* duties, outside of normal working hours. Certain duties that ended up with unfortunate consequences – and I don't just mean the increased frequency of Mrs Crawley's migraines.

---

* Going for dinner and not staying the night seems a bit uneconomical to be honest: the food ain't that good.

The maid found herself in a problematic condition, one which was, to say the least, quickly going to become difficult to conceal from the general public. Monte Cristo Homestead was not, at this time, a happy place to be, especially for the maid, but perhaps even more especially for Mrs Crawley. And it's likely that Mr Crawley wasn't feeling overly festive, either.

Now, what happened next is a matter of some conjecture. Some say that the maid, overwhelmed by the misery of her position, took a walk up to the house's balcony and threw herself off it. Others say that Mrs Crawley, overwhelmed by the misery of *her* position – and Mrs Crawley usually was – went up to the balcony, where the maid had just a minute earlier also gone, and gave the poor girl a quick shove.

Either way, the result was the same: the maid plummeted to the staircase below and met her violent end. The light patch on the step is where bleach was used to clean the girl's blood from the concrete – which is a charming detail that, as previously discussed, you can experience up close for fifteen bucks.

Far more interesting than a patch of bleached cement, though, is the maid herself. For one assumes it is she who has been seen walking along the verandah, to the spot where her life ended. Pale and silent and dressed immaculately in late Victorian style, she strolls back and forth, oblivious to all around her, recalling the terrible day when she either cracked under the pressure of middle-class morality, or cracked under the pressure of her employer's hand in the small of her back.

Notably, the maid does not appear inside the house, where Mrs Crawley's spirit seems to reign, putting the freeze on any intruders of whom she disapproves. With the mistress inside, it would appear that the poor maid has been barred from the warmth and comfort of the house, cursed to simply wander the grounds and contemplate her own death.

Visitors to Monte Cristo can also enjoy a walk up to the very balcony from which the maid fell. Feelings of vertigo have been reported in those who take that walk and look down on the yard: the balcony, it's said, gives one the feeling that it slopes down, as if trying to pitch anyone who stands on it over the rail.

When you take in the scene of the tragedy at Monte Cristo, you can't help but feel an overwhelming sadness, all the more so if you're lucky – or unlucky – enough to see the maid on her rounds, deaf and blind to the world's comforts. And yet this grim homestead has even more horrors to disgorge …

The Butcher of Adelaide Street

Brisbane, Queensland

The butcher's shop on Adelaide Street in the Brisbane CBD, just behind the Brisbane Arcade, is no more. Exactly where it stood, and whose shop it was, is forgotten. Some say it belonged to Patrick Mayne, an Irish immigrant who bought it with money stolen from a cedar cutter named Robert Cox – having earlier cut Cox into little pieces at the Bush Inn at Kangaroo Point. The tale of Mayne fits nicely with that of the Adelaide Street butcher, but whether they are the same story we can never really know.

But what we do know is that there was a butcher's shop, and it did a bustling trade, even though from time to time, without warning, employees and customers alike would be discomforted by something of a brouhaha.

It was a startling thing to witness. There was the butcher, chopping away. There was his assistant, wrapping a package of sausages for Mrs McDuff. There was Mrs McDuff, gratefully taking her sausages. There was an assortment of other customers, waiting for their own turn at a bit of meat and feeling vaguely resentful that only Mrs McDuff got a name in this story, even though she was just as imaginary as they were. The point is, everything was as it should be in this cosy temple of the flesh.

And then the peaceful, warm Brisbane air was rent by a distressing sound. From somewhere in the back of the shop came the noise of a ruckus. A voice raised in anger. Another one shouting a reply. A banging. A clanging. The sound of boots shuffling and of men scuffling. Yells and groans. A clatter. And then … a heart-stopping whoosh of air, as of something being hurled. Followed by a ghastly, wet, crunching *thunk*. A horrid, ungodly, truncated scream. The sound of something heavy thudding to the floor. And … silence.

The whole thing lasted less than a minute, but it felt like hours to the poor souls in the butcher's shop, who were frozen to the spot as they listened to it play out. The noises were utterly dreadful, such that it took nerves of tungsten for anyone to dare go into the back to have a look at the terrible aftermath of whatever had just transpired.

When finally someone did summon up the courage to bear witness to the gruesome scene, they found … nothing at all. Everything in the butcher's back room was as it should be, with nothing more disturbing than dozens of hanging animal corpses present.[*]

Nobody was there, and yet the sound of the backroom fight occurred again and again, giving the staff some pretty severe PTSD and scaring the daylights out of any number of customers (including, but not restricted to, Mrs McDuff). Funnily enough, discovering that there was nobody actually in the room didn't seem to comfort anyone: you'd think it was quite a relief to find out that no wild-eyed madman was about to burst out to repeat whatever bloody business he'd just carried out on the inhabitants of the shop. But somehow, the fact that the business had been heard, but no signs of it remained, was even more unnerving. People are odd like that.

Of course, there had been bloody business done in that room – many years before. Whether it was the sinister Mr Mayne or not, there was a butcher who had at one time fought with an underling and, in the course of the argument, lost his temper sufficiently to throw a meat cleaver, which embedded itself deep in the apprentice's skull, killing him stone dead. Whatever hideous mess had been left behind was soon cleaned up, but the echoes of the murder kept reverberating in the little

---

[*] Makes you think.

shop, so that generations hence, the sounds of the outrage continued to make themselves heard.

As I said, the butcher's shop is no longer there. No trace of the grisly fate of the butcher's apprentice remains. Unless, as you pass by the Brisbane Arcade one day, you listen closely, and try to block out the noise of the city. Then, there's just the slightest chance that, carried on the breeze, you may hear the faint remnants of the screams of more than a century ago.

The Man in Black

Kapunda, South Australia

The North Kapunda Hotel is Australia's most haunted pub, according to itself, and though it's only natural for any pub proprietor to want to lay claim to that title, the North Kapunda does have a decent claim. Earlier we met Dr Blood, the ludicrously perfectly named spirit of the long-gone respectable town doctor, mayor and mad scientist. But at the NK Hotel, Blood is only the beginning of the sinister goings-on.

It's happened many times to many guests of the hotel: whether there for a drink, staying in the rooms upstairs or, in latter days, visiting for the express purpose of getting spooked on a ghost tour. At some point, sitting at the bar or walking along the corridor, comes a voice: a rough, hate-filled snarl, barking in your ear: 'GET OUT!'

It's not a pleasant experience, but if that's the worst you get from your trip to North Kapunda, you may count yourself lucky. Because the ghost who just snarled in your ear was the Man in Black, and I don't mean Johnny Cash.* The Man in Black stalks the premises, in particular the upstairs corridor which the hotel's owners call the 'Hallway to Hell', and his raison d'etre seems to be to make life as unpleasant as possible for anyone who crosses his path.

He had a similar purpose in life, if tales are to be believed: the Man

---

* Though if you believe some of his songs, you don't want to run into him, either.

in Black is reputed to be the spirit of a vicious brute who, once upon a time, murdered a guest in one of the hotel's rooms. It is apparent that his own demise curtailed his homicidal career, and that in death, though frustrated by his insubstantial form and its inability to carry out actual murders, he strives to strike terror into the hearts of all he comes across. And he seems to target women in particular, so, you know, he's a real dick.

The Man in Black is easily recognised by the fact that his nickname is essentially accurate: he wears all black, with a wide-brimmed black hat that obscures his face, and he looms out of the shadows like a character in a Nick Cave song. His fury and bitterness towards the world of the living is quite clear when he rushes at unsuspecting guests and staff members, screaming. As mentioned, he prefers female targets, and many hapless women have been on the wrong end of a savage tirade or jump-scare, the Man in Black leaping from behind a door or around a corner to set a poor woman's heart to stopping. There is reason to believe he doesn't limit himself to scares, either: there are those who have felt a violent push pitch them forward, and others who report being scratched by long, sharp nails in the dark.

Nor does he restrict his terrorising to the living. Indeed, as there are plenty of other spirits haunting the North Kapunda Hotel – hence its 'most haunted' appellation – the Man in Black likes to keep busy menacing them as well. It's a rare and particularly obnoxious ghost who devotes his time to spooking spooks, but that's the Man in Black all over: a total jerk.

The other phantoms of the hotel have their own stories, which are told elsewhere in this very book, but their post-lives are blighted by the constant harassment of the Man in Black. Again, it's the female spirits who bear the brunt of his wrath. Sarah, a young girl who met her end tumbling over the hotel's balcony, is frequently stalked and bullied by the creep. Emily, a teen ghost who sits on the windowsill and looks down on the courtyard, has shut herself in one upstairs room for fear that she may run into the Man in Black if she wanders around the pub anymore.

Yes, though Australia's history is full of sad ghosts, angry ghosts, scary ghosts and even friendly ghosts, it can be said that the Man in Black at the North Kapunda Hotel is almost certainly the country's douchiest ghost.

The Evil Matron

Picton, New South Wales

There's just something about maternity hospitals, isn't there? I mean, not really, but if you go to a haunted one, you might start to think so. For yes, there is such a place, and once you hear its hair-whitening secrets you will forevermore consider *Carry On Matron* a horror movie.[*]

The potential of a maternity hospital for hauntings is underappreciated anyway, when you think of how haunted asylums usually are, and how a maternity hospital is basically just an asylum for mothers. And what's crazier than wanting to start a family, am I right, ladies? But seriously: if you want to know how terrifying an old maternity hospital can be, just think about babies.

Lots of babies.

Crying.

Screaming, sobbing, wailing.

In the night.

Even in a normal, currently operating hospital, if you had to work there it'd be enough to drive you mad and send you to an asylum, where you'd die and become a ghost. But imagine if the maternity hospital had not been operational for many years, but the sound of babies crying had never stopped.

---

[*] Fair play to you if you already do.

Creepy, right? I mean, what's scarier than the crying of a baby that isn't there? Admit it – that's the kind of thing that gets you burying your face in your date's shoulder at the movies. It's ironic that, in real life, a baby is one of the least dangerous creatures to encounter, yet a ghost baby is one of the most terrifying.

Which brings us to Picton. Just south-west of Sydney, this humble little burg is a nice place to stop on your way to more important places. There's a little picturesque scenery and some nice old buildings, and a few dozen ghosts knocking about the place. In fact, the tiny town may have the highest ratio of ghosts to living humans in all of Australia. And the old maternity hospital is one of their favourite hangouts.

The hospital is now a private residence, on the corner of Downing and Argyle streets, and if you happen to wangle an invitation, you will hear the sounds of those long-gone babies, crying through the night. Which is spooky as hell.* But you ain't seen nothing yet. Literally.

What life in the old maternity hospital was like back in the day, who can say? But it's safe to assume it wasn't a barrel of laughs, because the matron is still there, and she is not a cheerful Cheryl.

Many's the time an unfortunate person has awoken in fright from a hitherto peaceful slumber, gasping for breath and scrabbling at their throat, wondering what it is that is suddenly constricting their windpipe. They quickly realise the answer: hands. Cold, cruel hands, with bony fingers that curl around their neck and dig in hard. Choking and spluttering, the sleeper sits bolt upright, trying to tear the killer's hands from their throat, only to find there are no hands. It takes a few minutes for their breathing to return to normal, as you might expect.

The matron clearly does not appreciate people coming into her hospital who have no business there. Those who have walked the floors at the old maternity hospital know that she walks there too, sensible shoes clacking on the floorboards and her cold breath hissing down the backs of the unwelcome. The really unlucky have seen her face, flashing before them out of a dark room, creased with hate.

---

* Well, not as spooky as *hell*. I mean, that's quite a high bar.

Whether she was always this objectionable cannot be determined – perhaps death has made her more crotchety than she was originally – but it's a disturbing thought that this angry, bitter woman may, once upon a time, have pressed those bony fingers into innocent throats as they lay in their hospital beds. Or cribs …

The crying. It will not stop.

Caged Ghosts

Adelaide, South Australia

On the night of 24 March 1985, two eighteen-year-olds climbed the fence at Adelaide Zoo and went on a killing spree. Most of their slaughter was carried out in the children's zoo area, where they hacked to pieces rabbits, guinea pigs, turkeys, chickens, rhea chicks, a duck and a pigeon. They disembowelled sheep, stabbed goats and slashed the throats of kangaroos. They killed a llama and an antelope, and then moved on to the alligator enclosure. Here they bashed the huge but placid reptile over the head with an iron bar, shoved the bar into its eye, and finally disembowelled it and cut its foot off.

The director of the zoo said of the animals, 'Most of them were tame and would come up to you, and consequently were very easy to catch.' One of the teens said of the same animals, 'Some of them were running around, and the only way to stop them was to slash at them.' The young men ended up killing sixty-four animals, in as senseless a massacre as you could ever hope – or hope not – to see.

It's easy to imagine ghosts in a zoo. The spirits of the many animals who have lived and died on the grounds, for a start – particularly those who resided at such places in the bad old days, when zoos were collections of cruel, tiny cages and most of the animals lived miserable lives on cold concrete slabs. The era when orangutans were given cigarettes to smoke for the amusement of paying guests. It's also easy to imagine that even animals might want to get into the vengeful-spirit game after such terrible lives.

Moreover, a zoo – particularly at night – *sounds* haunted. The cries and whistles and croaks and growls that echo around an empty zoo in the dark are perfectly calculated to make the unconscious brain jump, thinking the shadows are full of hidden terrors.

But Adelaide Zoo, among all Australia's zoos, is the one where ghosts are more than just a jungle soundtrack. The 1985 slaughter was just the most shocking of a series of dark and dreadful happenings to have taken place there – the legacy of which remains to this day.

In 1920, zookeeper Samuel May, already a veteran of some nasty tangles with the creatures under his supervision, was hosing off a polar bear to keep it cool in the distinctly un-Arctic climate of South Australia. As he did so, the bear sidled up to the bars of its cage and suddenly lunged, reaching through the bars and tearing May's lower arm clean off. 'It is all up with me, I am gone!' cried May, as he collapsed in a pool of blood. The keeper was rushed to hospital, but he was right: he was gone.

The polar bear had taken some measure of revenge against the humans who confined it, and you'd have to think he was pretty satisfied with his day's work, even if Samuel May, who was after all only trying to make the animal more comfortable at the moment he was attacked, couldn't be said to the most deserving victim. In any event, it's the ghost of Sam May who, it's believed, still hangs around the zoo: his shadowy figure has been spotted close to where the bear swiped at him. Whether he's lingering for the love of the animals, to warn others about the unpredictable temperaments of polar bears, to beg forgiveness for his complicity in the poor treatment of animals in the early 20th century or just to look for his missing arm … anything's possible.

There has also been seen, at Minchin House, the original residence of the directors of the zoo, a woman in a long skirt and long sleeves, with her hair pulled back. Who knows who this might be, but perhaps she's a wife or daughter of an early zoo director, as she seems to be occupied with keeping watch over the residence.

But it's all those animals whose presence can be most keenly felt at Adelaide Zoo. The other-worldly echoes of wildlife past, filling the air with their own cries, communing with their living brethren and haunting the spaces of their own history.

The Ghost of Dog Trap Road

Parramatta, New South Wales

It was just after closing time that it happened. From the doors of the Vauxhall Inn, tucked into the bend of the railway line, a happy drinker staggered, saying his garbled goodbyes and bellowing a blessing to Mr Stone's famous buckets of rum.* Shuffling out onto Parramatta Road, the merry fellow blinked and looked about himself, trying to remember which direction was homeward. Slowly he began to weave his way down the road, leaving the warm puddle of light outside the Vauxhall and stumbling through the darkness before turning the corner.

And it was as he turned that the boisterous drunk was struck dumb with terror, falling to his knees and wailing aloud for help.

A dread shape was approaching, a huge, shimmering, white apparition, moaning and groaning as it bore down on the trembling pubgoer. 'OHHHHHHHHHHHHH,' it said. 'OOOOOOHHHHHHHHHHHHHHH!'

The man looked frantically around for anyone who could help him. There was no one. He was alone and helpless to defend himself against the looming spectre.

Some time later, the petrified punter was shaken awake by passers-by,

---

* Innkeeper Stone had advertised 'a bucket of rum for a penny', and then unveiled his custom-made 'buckets': the size of a wineglass, solid wood, with a depression in the top sufficient for a teaspoon of rum. They were wildly popular. Seriously. Real fact.

curled in a ball and moist in an unfortunate way. Just the latest victim of the ghost of Dog Trap Road.

There were dozens of testimonies as to the bloodcurdling nature of the spectre, the terrible sounds it made, the hideous hollow eyes with which it stared at you as it floated out of hell to lay you dead from fright upon the cobbles. All who witnessed it came out of the experience in a state of gibbering shock, and would've needed a stiff drink (if they hadn't pretty much all had several already).

The ghost always appeared in the Dog Trap Road vicinity, near the Vauxhall Inn, favourite watering hole of the Stone Push. The Stone Push was a gang of larrikins in the 1870s, when 'larrikin' meant 'violent criminal' rather than 'beloved sporting champion'. The Stone Push was a rowdy and rambunctious lot, but its members were not as menacing as the Rocks Push, who ruled the streets of Sydney and slashed throats for relaxation.

The Stone Push's tastes ran more to pranks and practical jokes. One of their favourites was, late at night, after leaving the pub, one of their number would get dressed up in a big sheet and jump out at unsuspecting people heading home, making spooky moaning noises and pretending to be a terrifying ghost.

Savvy readers will have noticed a certain dovetailing of the narrative at this point.

Yes, the ghost of Dog Trap Road, unlike all the other ghosts in this book,* was a definite fake, just some incorrigible youths having a laugh at the expense of the vulnerable and easily confused. It was despicable behaviour really, frightening people half to death just for a few cheap laughs. On the other hand, it must have been really funny at the time.

But fun, unlike ghosts, does not last forever. Suspicion started to grow among the burghers of Parramatta that something hinky was going on, and a few of them resolved to do something about it. One young man in particular, a shopkeeper of Crown Street, got a couple of mates together, and the three of them hatched a devilishly clever plan.

---

* I swear to god!

The plan, as intricate as clockwork, was this: grab hold of the Stone Push dickheads and beat the crap out of them.

It was almost too brilliant.

So it was that on one dark, foggy night, as the ghost of Dog Trap Road stepped out to wreak more horror, he was set upon by three burly fellows who tore the sheet off him and proceeded to give him, in the words of contemporary reports, 'a good horse-whipping'.* The sheeted chap's companions, who were loitering nearby, came in for a few lashes of their own.

And so was the ghost of Dog Trap Road vanquished, and the patrons of the Vauxhall Inn made safe once more, and Parramatta breathed a sigh of relief.

---

* If a horse-whipping can ever be described as 'good'.

Night at the Railway Museum

Port Adelaide, South Australia

So, you think a railway museum is pretty boring, eh kids? You think it's 'uncool' and 'square' and 'cringe'? I know what you're saying. You're saying, 'Who wants to go to a stupid old building and look at stupid old trains when I could be playing Pokémon Go or making TikToks or watching hit Australian cartoon *Bluey?*'*

Well, let me hit you with some knowledge, youngsters: the National Railway Museum at Port Adelaide is not your average boring railway museum. You have to visit at night, though. When you visit the NRM in the dark, you find a place that is a far cry from the dust-covered Isle of Sodor you're imagining: a place where the emphasis is less on trains and more on a history of horrible grisly death and the other-worldly ripples that history continues to leave in the fabric of our own reality.

So how's THAT for 'cringe'?

The first thing you have to know about the National Railway Museum is that it is built on the site of a former railway station and goods yard at Port Adelaide: a site at which there were at least twenty-one reported deaths. Occupational health and safety was pretty lax back then, but even so it's an impressive body count, with the deaths including the accidents you might expect on a railway as well as ... dun dun DUN ... murder!

---

* I do not meet a lot of young people.

So the place had a pretty nasty energy before the museum even sprang up there, and when it did it took that energy on and made it its own. A good start was acquiring the locomotive involved in the Battle of Broken Hill, Australia's first terrorist attack. On 1 January 1915, two men opened fire on a train from Broken Hill to Silverton, killing four people. That's the engine that's now proudly displayed at the NRM, and which really adds to the whole 'Museum of Death' vibe.

Whether the shadowy figures who scuttle around the building at night include any of the victims of the terrorist attack, or they're all the spirits of those who departed the world of the living at the old station, they do seem to possess a certain interest in the museum's exhibits. When the night-time ghost tours come through – combining good solid scares with fascinating facts about steam power, tickets on sale now – the shadows tend to follow them, meaning visitors are constantly hearing footsteps behind them and looking around to see indistinct figures ducking out of sight or hiding in dark corners.

Other apparitions have been seen walking along the platforms in the museum, or in the trains themselves, wandering through the carriages or peeking out of windows at passers-by, who have understandably reported feeling 'kind of weird' about this. Feeling weird seems to be a part of the experience of visiting the museum, in fact: huge mood swings are a likely symptom of being inside the NRM.

But if you can survive the emotional highs and lows, and you don't mind having the eyes of a few dozen dead people on you as you make your way through the museum, you can take a walk, accompanied by the eerie disembodied whistling of an invisible yet jaunty fellow, to the jewel in the NRM's crown: the haunted brake van.

In here you will encounter something, or someone. The identity of the entity is unknown, but what *is* known is that it is very angry, and it's going to take its anger out on you. If you can stay in the brake van for longer than a minute without running out in panic, then you truly are the bravest of trainspotters.

The Black Horse of Sutton Forest

Sutton Forest, New South Wales

It was in the days of the wild colonial boys, when Sutton Forest was not yet grand enough to aspire to the title of 'village'. When the rolling green hills were unspoiled by grey roads, and the lawns of Captain Nicholson's house were immaculate. It was in the days when even an outlaw could have a quiet drink at the Heritage Hotel, for they'd not be bothered there. Nobody came to Sutton Forest.

But the black horse – yes, the black horse came to Sutton Forest. It came galloping past the church. It came thundering past the Heritage Hotel. It came hurtling past the other church. It wasn't in Sutton Forest long – you can't be in Sutton Forest for very long unless you walk really slowly – but it was long enough for the locals to peek through their windows, roused by the sudden ominous thrumming of hooves across the dirt, and see the flash of sleek flanks in the moonlight, a mane flying in the night breeze.

At first, it was assumed that the black horse was … well, a black horse. Call the people of Sutton Forest naive country bumpkins, but that was the way of things back then: the bush bred the sort of literal-mindedness that would cause a bloke to see a horse and say, 'That's a horse,' without any kind of self-interrogation as to the internal biases that led to such a conclusion. You can't really blame them: it takes a while to break out of your mental programming to consider that the horse you just saw cantering past the pub was possibly a spectral apparition sent from the depths of the nether dimensions to prophesy impending doom. Especially if this is the first spectral apparition sent from the depths of the nether dimensions to prophesy impending doom that you've seen: and for most Sutton Foresters, it was.

The first clue that something was not quite right with the black horse was linked to the fact that, though it was seen more than once rushing down the main street, nobody could ever find it afterwards. In daylight they searched the surrounding woods and plains, but of that magnificent stallion – and it was magnificent, with the glossiest of coats, the thickest of manes, a proud head and perfect form – there was never a sign. The men would try to chase it as it rushed through in the night, but always the horse would vanish into the shadows beyond the town, too fast for any pursuers.

The second clue that something was not quite right with the black horse came on the evening it bolted down the main street only to find a wagon standing in its way. A lifetime's experience had taught the men of Sutton Forest that when a horse finds a wagon standing in its way, the normal thing for it to do is to go around it. So when the black horse chose instead to pass straight *through* the wagon, coming out the other side with seemingly no ill effects, they were absolutely certain that something was up. It became a common sight: the horse racing through the town, passing through solid objects and buildings without breaking stride.

A common sight, and a terrifying one: not only was seeing a horse run through an outhouse distinctly unnerving, but word got around Sutton Forest that when the animal made an appearance, misfortune followed hard on its hooves. A drought or a flood, a deadly snakebite, a bad batch of beer at the Heritage Hotel, rain on your wedding day, 10,000 spoons when all you need is a knife … Many and varied were the catastrophes that occurred in the wake of the black horse.

To this day, where that horse came from and where it went to are a mystery. The spirit of a long-dead steed, taking revenge on mistreatment in life by bringing misfortune upon humanity? Or warning the townsfolk of impending disaster to make amends for horsey sins during its life? Or maybe the horse never was alive: it was simply an everyday common or garden demon horse, such as we are all familiar with? All we can know for sure is that it must've been pretty cool to see it.

Grover's Ghost

Richmond, Tasmania

George Grover had been sent to Tasmania as punishment for stealing – which was a very harsh punishment, but from all accounts Grover was a real jerk, so he probably deserved it. He had a reputation for aggression and general obnoxiousness, which made it unsurprising that after he served his sentence, he took a job as a whip-bearer on chain gangs. It was a dick move, and therefore George Grover all over.

With whip in hand, Grover was a holy terror, flogging the daylights out of the hapless convicts employed to carry sandstone from the quarry at Butcher's Hill to the bridge at Richmond, which was being rebuilt. If a convict misbehaved in any way, Grover would whip him. If a convict did not misbehave in any way, Grover would whip him. He would sit on the stones as they were dragged along, whipping the men all the way. He was nothing if not consistent, and the authorities saw a lot to like in his All Whipping All The Time approach, giving him more money and more power. Grover was in his element, living his lifelong dream of getting paid to violently abuse men who were, effectively, his slaves. He loved his life.

But as the ancient Greeks taught us, beware hubris! Or as the ancient Greeks might've put it if they'd been around in 19th-century Australia: beware booze. George Grover failed to take this advice – which to be

118

fair he'd never actually heard, since it was a purely hypothetical warning in a book written nearly two hundred years after he died – and one night got roaring drunk.

It's probably not going to astound you to learn that Grover was not a pleasant drunk. So unpleasant was he, in fact, that his neighbours, on the farm where his modest hut was located, turfed him off the property. Stumbling inebriated through Richmond, Grover eventually came to rest on the bridge, where he fell asleep – a tactical error, as it turned out.

The convicts who had been working on Richmond Bridge under Grover's sadistic stewardship found the sleeping man and got stuck into some good old-fashioned revenge. Grover woke to a flurry of kicks and punches, and was in no condition to defend himself. The convicts, delirious with joy at being able to give their overseer a hefty dose of his own medicine, threw themselves into their work with gusto. The coup de grâce came when one enterprising convict slammed a pickaxe into Grover's head, following which his comrades hoisted the well-tenderised man up and over the side of the bridge and into the cold Coal River below.

That was the end of George Grover's reign of terror – over the convict workers, anyway. Those who frequent the Richmond area and have an aversion to ghosts might still find themselves somewhat oppressed by Grover, who in spectral form continues to make a nuisance of himself. Sometimes you may see him walking across the bridge, possibly ruminating on the virtues of temperance. Other times he simply stands by the bridge, staring at you until you feel awkward and go away.

Not that that will necessarily help you, because George Grover is such a knob-end that he doesn't even stick to haunting the place of his violent death like a decent ghost: sometimes he follows people home and haunts their houses, which to me is just taking a liberty in the worst way. If you should be unfortunate enough to run into Grover's ghost, be prepared for him to harangue and berate you: he's as aggressive and unpleasant as he was in life; but it is important to remember that he can't whip anyone anymore, making his bark a hell of a lot worse than his bite.

Far friendlier is the ghost of a black dog known as 'Grover's dog', for reasons of bankrupt imagination. Despite the name appended to it, Grover's dog doesn't seem particularly loyal to the deceased whip-bearer: the jolly little pup is actually believed to hang around Richmond Bridge to warn people that Grover is about. Funnily enough, the dog *doesn't* seem to follow people back to their houses, but if you can coax him into your car, I'm sure he'd love a Forever Home. Just don't accidentally let Grover hitch a ride at the same time, because you know he'll make the drive home a living hell.

The Haunted Arcade

Chapter One
Adelaide, South Australia

If you take a stroll through the Adelaide Arcade, you can even now sometimes hear the strains of 'The Adelaide Arcade Grand Polka', the tune composed for the occasion of the arcade's opening, ringing out on the piano accordion.* It's a merry old tune, and quite at odds with the history of Australia's oldest shopping arcade: that history being one filled with tragedy, murder and paranormal freakiness.

The arcade, when it was built in 1885, was a marvel of the age, particularly in Australia, where people were still getting used to the idea of ceilings. An opulent confection of marble and glass, with a grand internal staircase, fountains and even a Turkish bath in which one could pay four shillings to become clean in an Eastern fashion, it was a marvellous testament to the colony of South Australia and its motto, 'We Have More Money Than You'.

Although every shop in the arcade had a gaslight outside the door – which came in handy when shopkeepers had to convince customers that they'd already received their change and must be imagining things – the building was one of the first in Adelaide to have electric light. The lights were maintained by a man named Henry Hardcourt, and when Henry wasn't around, the arcade's caretaker, a fellow called

---

* All public spaces in Adelaide are required to have a designated piano-accordion player as a matter of law.

Francis Cluney, took responsibility for them.

Two years after the arcade opened, Cluney had been left in charge when the electric lights started flickering. Often, the flickering of lights is a sign of paranormal activity …

TWIST! It wasn't a ghost at all, it was just faulty lights. Understandably, Francis, who was thoroughly devoted to duty, went to see what the trouble was. Observers would have been disappointed that whatever the trouble was, Francis clearly wasn't able to fix it, because shortly after he left the lights went out entirely.

At this point readers might be crying, 'What the hell? Why, having purchased* a book of ghost stories, am I suddenly reading this piffling drivel about electrical faults?'

Well, for the love of god, calm down, because there's another TWIST coming.

The lights hadn't gone out because of a blown fuse or a broken wire. No, the reason that darkness had suddenly descended on the Adelaide Arcade was that the body of Francis Cluney was stuck inside the generator. It's possible that someone pushed him, or it's possible that the official inquest, which heard that his clothes had got caught in the machinery, dragging him in, was on the right track. Whatever the cause, Cluney died as horrendously gruesome a death as a man could: chewed up and mangled by the remorseless metal monster.

If anyone had cause to be aggrieved with his lot in life – or, rather, in death – it was Francis Cluney, so nobody can blame him for continuing to hang around the arcade making his presence felt. Those who have just moved into their premises at the arcade are particularly prone to sightings of the dutiful gentleman: he clearly likes to greet new faces. Occasionally he knocks things over, just to let you know he's around. Sometimes he'll mess about with electrical items, no doubt considering that he and electricity have unfinished business.

The most startling appearances of Cluney, however, come in the form of the man himself, complete and immaculate in his long coat,

---

* You did purchase it, right? Shame on you.

walking the shiny arcade floors, looking curiously into shop windows and watching shoppers from the balcony above. Dedicated to the arcade in life, he remains so in death, and as unsettling as it must be to see him gliding about the place, there's something rather touching about the way he insists on keeping an eye on his beloved place of work, even now.

The Haunted Arcade

Chapter Two
Adelaide, South Australia

Francis Cluney's is far from the only tragic tale to come out of the Adelaide Arcade. One could easily refer, for example, to Thomas Horton, the bootmaker and amateur juggler, who, after falling out of a tree as a child, grew up to be a violent monster who shot his estranged wife in Arcade Lane – after she had predicted just such an occurrence in writing. But though Thomas lies even now in the grounds of Adelaide Gaol, his spirit has not yet given anyone any trouble.

A similarly tragic but more phantasmic story is that of Bridget Kennedy Byron, a fortune teller who, in the early 1900s, operated out of a shop in the arcade that she shared with her husband, Professor Kennedy. The professor was a phrenologist, and many was the night the Kennedys would stay up late arguing about whose profession was the more ludicrous. Eventually, Professor Kennedy, unable to stand life with a woman whose charlatanism could match his own, left Bridget for another woman, taking their little boy Sydney with him.

Bridget, strangely enough not relying on her own psychic powers, got Sydney back with the help of a private detective, but 'happily ever after' just wasn't in the cards* for this poor woman. One day in the Adelaide Arcade, the smell of gas was detected and traced to Bridget's shop, where mother and son lay beside each other: Bridget senseless and Sydney, alas, dead.

---

* Fun little psychic joke there, keeping it light.

Bridget was charged with the murder of her son, but acquitted – despite the fact that she had, the day before he died, dictated a note to his nanny that read in part, 'Tired of life; heart is broken ... Let my baby and myself go to the students to the hospital [*sic*].' Despite this, the judge found that no jury could convict on the available evidence: possibly because of the testimony of a Dr Hines that Bridget was 'mentally unhinged'.

But as one might imagine, her life did not at this point make the smooth transition to peaches and cream. Husband gone and child buried, she turned to drink and fell, quite understandably, apart. It almost seemed a blessed relief when her body was found in Adelaide's West Parklands; though any suspicion of a peaceful death was scotched by the discovery that she'd been poisoned.

Nobody knows whether Bridget Kennedy Byron was murdered, committed suicide or was simply the victim of a terrible accident, as she had for some time been self-medicating with alcohol and a variety of drugs. But whatever the cause of her sad end, she may well be seeking justice – or redemption – still, if we are to credit the reports of a female ghost walking the floors of the arcade. Some have even seen her wandering along beside the tall, distinguished figure of Francis Cluney, presumably swapping stories of cursed luck. And then there are ... the other stories.

For the shopkeepers of the Adelaide Arcade have often heard the footsteps of children running at all hours of the day and night, and visitors have felt their sleeves being tugged and their hands grabbed, as if a small child were endeavouring to get their attention. A small child, perhaps, who wished to set the record straight about the black cloud of suspicion that still hangs over his mother's head more than a century after her death ...

Even more chillingly, investigators have recorded in the Adelaide Arcade the voice of a child that came out of thin air: a voice that could, if permitted as evidence in a court of law, possibly prove Bridget Kennedy Byron's innocence. Sadly, the recorded voices of ghost children are not yet considered admissible evidence in most jurisdictions, so Bridget's name has not yet been cleared. And yet it is both moving and sort of terrifying to think that little Sydney Kennedy Byron is still doing his best to let the world know that his mother was a far better woman than the world was led to believe during her lifetime.

Mad Dan Morgan

Woodend, Victoria

There is no doubt that, in a profession in which a little madness was almost mandatory to make a man want to sleep in the dirt and constantly flee from armed police, Daniel Morgan was the maddest bushranger of all. His insanity went well beyond the basic craziness required to make the bushranging life seem appealing, into the kind of wild-eyed derangement that meant that when a movie was made about him, Dennis Hopper was the go-to guy for the lead role.

Mad Dan Morgan – also known as William John Owen, John Smith, Dan Moran, William Morgan, Big Morgan, Bill the Native, 'Down the River Jack' and 'the Terror of the Riverina'* – terrorised southern New South Wales for a couple of years in the 1860s, gaining a reputation for brutality and unpredictability. He was the kind of man who would give you a hug and buy you a drink two minutes before shooting you in the neck because your smile reminded him of a man who'd once stolen his watch. He had an unusually high turnover in accomplices, because there were few men who could ride for long with Mad Dan Morgan before running away gibbering into the bush.

It was when he decided to expand his horizons by crossing into Victoria, though, that Morgan finally met his match. After taking the inhabitants of Peechelba Station hostage, Morgan partied all night,

---

* It was a golden age for aliases.

drinking heavily and getting the ladies of the homestead to play piano for him. Waking to the news that the house was surrounded and his goose quite deliciously cooked, Morgan took it well, retreating to a bedroom to do his hair and beard nicely, before marching out of the house to get shot.

Photographs of Morgan's body just after his death show a fearsome visage, with long hair, a wild black beard, piercing eyes and an expression that seems to say, 'I'll be back to getcha.' Besides being ambushed and shot in the back, Morgan had plenty to be aggrieved about in his death: spectators gathered round and began taking locks of his hair home as keepsakes. Officials then cut off his beard, shaved his head and decapitated him. It was not very dignified, to say the least.

Bushrangers' ghosts are not nearly as plentiful as you might expect in Australia: perhaps because most bushrangers, once dead, were happy to concede that they'd had the time of their lives and really had no regrets about the way their chosen career had abbreviated their life span. Mad Dan Morgan was quite another kettle of blood: he left this world knowing he had a lot more marauding in him, and that there was a whole mess of revenge left untaken.

This is why around Woodend, in Victoria, people say that the hideous headless horseman who rides over the hills at night is the ghost of Dan Morgan, forever trying to get some more bushranging in. Driven by a seething sense of resentment at the fact that death could not apparently get his head back from authorities, Mad Dan gallops out from Hanging Rock, which was rumoured to be his hideout until all those schoolgirls started snooping around. An underground stream there runs red with rust, causing it to be dubbed 'Morgan's Blood'. It's apt that the countryside should be soaked with Morgan's blood, given the amount of blood he spilled himself.

The tragedy of Morgan, of course, is that as a ghost all he seems able to do is ride about the mountains with his head cut off, looking for people he can wave his gun at; and he will therefore most likely never fulfil his bushranging dreams. Of course, some might say the tragedy of Morgan is that he was killed at the age of thirty-four, and there's something in that. But most thirty-four-year-olds don't have quite as much bloodlust to satisfy, so it's apples and oranges.

Just keep an eye out if you're around Woodend way: the dude, we must stress, is quite, quite mad.

The Governor's Ghost

Brisbane, Queensland

There are those who believe that, of all the Australian states, Queensland is arguably one of the best half-dozen. There is the weather, for a start, and also other things. But perhaps the most compelling evidence that Queensland is, to use the phrase adopted as an official motto by a completely different state, 'the place to be' is that the ghost of its first governor, Sir George Ferguson Bowen, continues to haunt Old Government House in the grounds of Brisbane's Queensland University of Technology.

For Brisbane was not, it must be emphasised, where Sir George died. He perished peacefully at the age of seventy-seven in Brighton, England, and was laid to rest at Kensal Green Cemetery in London. He might easily have chosen to haunt the green lawns of Kensington, but he did not.

Before he made his way to Queensland in 1859, Bowen served as the chief secretary to the government of the Ionian Islands, a tiny group of Greek islands that had come under British rule due to a typo. But although the Ionian Islands are an exceedingly pleasant, balmy spot, with lovely beaches and palm trees all over the place, he did not decide to spend his post-mortem years spooking the Ionians.

After his stint in Brisbane, Sir George's career took him even further afield. He was Governor of New Zealand from 1868 to 1873, Governor of Victoria from 1873 to 1879, Governor of Mauritius from 1879 to 1883, and Governor of Hong Kong, China from 1883 to 1887. Yet none of these places appealed enough to him to tempt him to haunt them.

No, it was Queensland, where Sir George was governor from 1859 to 1868, that his ghost chose to make his final restless place. It is there, on the stairs in Old Government House, that he has been seen on many an occasion, walking with magisterial deliberation up and also down, decked out in his splendid robes of office, his magnificent mutton-chops serving as a reminder to modern generations that, once upon a time in this country, there was such a thing as standards: back in the days when the British Empire would no more allow a man without spectacular sideburns to assume a vice-regal position than they would grant an indigenous population self-determination.

It's said that as Sir George walks the stairs in Old Government House, he nods to himself in a thoughtful manner, as though weighing the relative merits of some crucial question of colonial governance and deriving satisfaction from the conclusions he has drawn. Maybe he's pondering the financial crisis of 1866, in which he famously* refused to issue inconvertible paper money. Or maybe he's thinking about something less boring. But concerned with hefty affairs of state the ghost most assuredly is, and the specific issue doesn't really matter.

What's important is that anyone can go to Old Government House and see Sir George Ferguson Bowen in all his whiskery glory. It's a far more stirring experience than looking at a mere painting of the statesman, for, as the saying goes, a picture's worth a thousand words, but a ghost is worth at least forty or so pictures. Seeing Queensland's first governor in the ectoplasm makes for an incredibly educational experience for any student of history.

Because unlike ghosts who scare, ghosts who sadden and ghosts who threaten, the ghost of Sir George Ferguson Bowen performs a very

---

* 'Famously' is a relative term, of course.

different and far more comforting role. He keeps us mindful of the grandeur of government, and the fact that, no matter how intimidating and frustrating modern life might get, there is always someone watching over us.

Mind you, he's also pretty bloody scary when you see him up close.

The Old Lady at Elizabeth Farm

Rosehill, New South Wales

Elizabeth Farm, at Rosehill in Sydney, is a house positively bulging at the seams with history. It was built for the young couple John and Elizabeth Macarthur in 1793, when John was a dashing young army officer with big dreams of becoming a wealthy megalomaniac, and Elizabeth was a beautiful young wife with big dreams of becoming a less beautiful old wife.

As John's wealth grew, and the governor continued giving him more grants of land in return for John's help converting the army into an organised crime syndicate, the little cottage expanded to become a large and picturesque homestead, the centre of the sheep-breeding operation that made the family's name and fortune. John Macarthur would go down in history as a pioneer of wool, one of the most prominent men in early New South Wales and a violent criminal who went insane. Elizabeth Macarthur would go down in history as a strong, intelligent woman with a hell of a lot of patience.

Today, Elizabeth Farm is an 'access-all-areas' museum, meaning you can walk through it and see it just as it was in the Macarthurs' day, and touch everything with your dirty, sticky fingers and probably break stuff, which is fine because it's all fake anyway. It's a lot of fun to take your whole family for a stroll around Elizabeth Farm and look out for the exact moment your children lose the will to live.

But a visit to Elizabeth Farm doesn't have to be all tedium and whingeing ten-year-olds. For example, you could have a Devonshire tea, or, as the official website helpfully advises, you can 'smell the herbs in the kitchen garden'. You can see how that could be fun, right?

Or, of course, you could try to spot the ghost. She's not a friendly ghost, but nor is she an angry one. She's of the category known by ghostologists as 'aloof', and she will probably pay no attention to you at all: even if you stand right in front of her, it's likely she will walk straight through you, giving you a moment of terrible icy dread and an aftertaste of Devonshire tea.

The old lady of Elizabeth Farm is just there to look after the place, to make sure everything is in order. In all likelihood she hates it when you lay your grubby mitts all over the replica tablecloths, and winces when she sees you dragging the chairs across the floor and scuffing up their feet. Her disapproving looks are quite in line with the tasteful decor and understated Georgian vibe of the house in general. There is nothing flashy about the old lady: she is there to do a job, and that job is to appear fleetingly in mirrors or at the end of corridors, long skirts rustling as she checks that nothing is out of place.

Who is the old lady? I'm glad you asked. It could be Eleanor Killpack – referred to as 'poor old Nelly Killpack' by Elizabeth Macarthur – whose first husband, David Killpack, had worked as a farm manager for the Macarthurs. David died in 1797 and Nelly remarried, but she stayed in the Macarthurs' employ for over four decades; she was still using the name Killpack in 1842. There's every chance that Nelly, who stuck with the Macarthurs through thick and thin for so many years, saw fit to stay on at the farm after she passed away, just to make sure things were still exactly as the master and mistress would like it.

But it also could be Sarah Pettit, the woman who was at Elizabeth Farm from the very start, having come over with the Macarthurs on the Second Fleet in 1790. Sarah helped to look after their baby son on that voyage, and was nurse to more Macarthur children born in Sydney. In 1807, she left New South Wales with her husband to return to England, and in later years ran into John Macarthur Junior, who had once been under her care. She told him that she wished she could return to Elizabeth Farm.

Perhaps, after passing away, Sarah Pettit did just that, coming back to the house where she had taken charge of its youngest inhabitants, to the place in the world where she felt most at home. Perhaps she is there still.

The Road to Capalaba

Brisbane, Queensland

Maybe it's simply that one's eyes can play tricks on one. Maybe it's the power of suggestion on a tired brain at the end of a long day. Maybe we have all heard too many stories of ghosts and apparitions, or too many songs about young lovers in tragic accidents on the road. Maybe there's nothing there at all. I can't say for sure what's out there; all I can tell you is what people have seen. And what people have seen is terrible and frightening and bizarre.

It was on the road to Capalaba, heading east from Mount Gravatt in Brisbane's south. Around Wishart, near the Broadwater Road intersection, where the highway begins to bend from north-east to east as it crosses Bulimba Creek. You drive through the green parklands on that stretch of road, then come to the Gateway Motorway. Of course, the motorway wasn't always there. Certainly the … 'vision' was around long before the motorway, though not before the road itself. The road must have been there, or it couldn't … well, you'll see.

You drive east on the road to Capalaba, and it's late in the day, and the sun is setting behind you as you drive, and the heat of a Brisbane day is just beginning to fade. And you rub your eyes because you're tired and you're hot and you're looking forward to the end of your journey. And stretching out before you, the road shimmers just a little as the sun inches towards the horizon, and though it's knocking-off time for

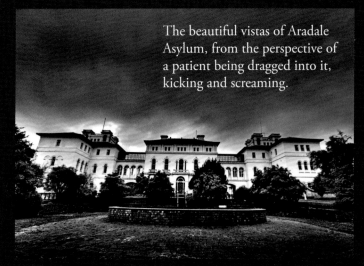

The beautiful vistas of Aradale Asylum, from the perspective of a patient being dragged into it, kicking and screaming.

The unfortunate John Farley meets Fisher's Ghost, in one of his moods.

The Port Arthur Historical Precinct, where anyone can have a fun day celebrating colonial atrocities.

Adelaide Gaol, sending out an ominous warning to anyone who, for some reason, doesn't already find prisons ominous.

This sculpture can be found beside the Cobb Highway, and depicts the Headless Horseman of Black Swamp frantically trying to return a waffle iron to a close friend.

Oakabella Homestead, auditioning for a lead role in *Wolf Creek 3*.

Larundel Asylum, showing off its brand-new avant-garde decor.

Notorious bushranger Mad Dan Morgan, pictured shortly after his death, mulling over the pros and cons of ghosthood.

Cell 17 of Old Melbourne Gaol, currently listed at $1.2 million on realestate.com.au.

Death masks at Melbourne Gaol, revealing the amazing fact that all criminals in 19th century Australia were bald men without pupils.

George Bowen, first governor of Queensland, photographed seconds after being told that he was, in fact, a ghost.

The Old Lady at Elizabeth Farm, pictured here being invisible.

THE LATE MR. F. BAKER (FEDERICI).

Opera singer Federici, who haunts Melbourne's Princess Theatre, terrifying unwary theatregoers with his nitpicking criticisms of *Hamilton*.

The bedroom of 'Sarah' at the North Kapunda Hotel, where legend says anyone who spends the night becomes overwhelmed with a desire to redecorate.

The forbidding facade of Graham's Castle, still the spookiest thing to be associated with anyone called Graham.

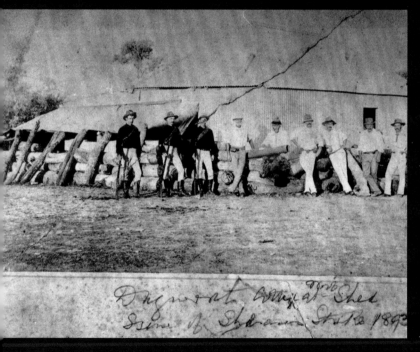

Troopers at Dagworth Station during the shearers' strike of 1894, later to inspire the lyrics to 'Waltzing Matilda' and, by extension, the self-delusion of several generations of Australians.

A dummy in Albany Convict Gaol, specially placed so that any ghosts you might meet will seem tame by comparison.

the whole city, just for a moment it seems as though you're all on your lonesome, for the road ahead seems clear. And then you see something.

It's nothing, though. It's just a burst of light, the sun glinting off metal somewhere in front of you. For a second it blinds you, but there's no harm done as you drive on. But as you get closer to the spot where the flash came from, you begin to see what it is.

The low sun has bounced off the visor of a helmet, worn by a man who is kneeling on the road. You slow as you approach, pulling over just short of him. A little further down the road you see a motorbike, lying on its side. The man, all in leather, clearly its rider, has survived the crash in decent shape. Indeed, he is showing no ill effects, as far as you can see. The same cannot be said for his companion.

It's a young woman in a summer dress. She is lying ominously still in the middle of the highway, and the man in the helmet is kneeling over her prone form. His hands are reaching out to her … to see if she's alive? Or …

Just for a moment, the man looks up from the woman and turns his face towards you. The sun once again glints off his visor. He turns back to the woman.

In a panic, you open the door and leap out of your car, calling out to the man, asking what happened, offering your assistance. But as your door slams shut and you hurry to help, you stop dead in your tracks, and you blink, and you stare.

For the man, and the woman, and the motorbike … are not there.

You have just seen them, as plain as the nose on your face. But now they are nowhere to be seen. The road stretches away into the distance, ahead and behind you. The parklands stretch away on either side. There is nowhere anyone could have disappeared to – certainly nowhere that a man and a woman with a motorbike could have got away to in the time between you stopping your car and getting out. They have simply vanished, or they were never there at all.

You rub your eyes. You are tired and hot. The sun is blood-red in the west. You look one way up the highway, then the other. You slowly walk back to your car. Get in, start up and pull out onto the road, where you are soon once more in the thick of busy traffic.

And you drive home, knowing what you saw and knowing that you could not have. And the sun sets over the road to Capalaba.

The Spooks of Monte Cristo

Part Three

Junee, New South Wales

We return, once again, to our beloved Monte Cristo Homestead, the Junee house where it's all ghosts, all the time, or your money back. We know of the unhappy Mrs Crawley, and the even less happy maid who went headlong over the balcony and onto the steps below. But the horrors of the homestead don't stop there. They don't even stop at the house itself.

The stables at Monte Cristo give off a foul energy: visitors have said they can't even bring themselves to go near them, such is the dread radiating from the building. This may be connected to the stable boy who once worked there, who was burned alive in his bed by his master. Today, that stable boy's melancholy presence can be felt in the coach-house.

But for something really disturbing, the kind of thing that will keep ping-ponging around your brain for weeks and make the fifteen bucks you paid to visit Monte Cristo well worthwhile – for that, you'll want to head to the caretaker's cottage. There, beside the doorway, you'll find a short rusty chain hanging from the wall, and a deep groove in the wall where the chain attaches to it. This chain belonged to Harold.

Harold was the son of the housekeeper of Monte Cristo, once upon a time. As a child, Harold was discovered to be intellectually disabled, although you can be pretty sure that wasn't the term they used at the time. It was a far less enlightened era when it came to disabilities, so the love and support one might expect a child like Harold to receive today was not granted to the poor lad. Instead, going by the most cutting-edge medical and psychological advice available at the time, they decided to help Harold to lead a rich and fulfilling life by chaining him to a wall.

While his mother worked in the house, Harold would stay, on that short chain, alone in the cottage. Nothing to do but pace back and forth, just as far as his metal leash would let him – which wasn't far at all. The groove in the wall is where Harold wore away the brickwork with his chain, dragging it up and down, day after day … for forty years.

Yes. Forty years. For forty years Harold lived on the end of that chain, forbidden from leaving the cottage or seeing anyone but his family, whose shame at his presence was so overwhelming. For forty years, his mother kept her son from the world, shackled like a dog.

When the housekeeper died, they found her lying in the cottage, with Harold curled up at her feet. Harold was unchained and sent to a home for the insane, where he too soon passed away. And then … he came back.

Free at last, Harold now roams the grounds of the Monte Cristo Homestead. He's looking for his mother, who left him so many years ago with no explanation that he could understand. He's looking for answers about what has happened to him, and to the house. He's looking for a friend … maybe you?

So don't be scared when you're in the yard at Monte Cristo and you hear the clanking of chains being dragged towards you across the stones. Don't be afraid as they get louder and louder, the closer Harold comes to you. Don't be frightened when the chains stop clanking and you feel hot, heavy breath on your neck. Don't be terrified when you feel a hand grab for yours, or when you hear a whisper in your ear.

Harold was so lonely for forty years … He's just happy that you're here … and that you'll be friends forever.

The Phantom of the …
You Know

Melbourne, Victoria

Opening night, Princess Theatre, Melbourne, 3 March 1888. The cream of society was in attendance to see Charles Gounod's opera *Faust*, with orchestra conducted by Alfred Cellier. Clarence 'Jack' Leumane was in the title role, and Nellie Stewart played Marguerite, but the star attraction of the production was the acclaimed Italian-born English bass-baritone Frederick Federici,* in the role of Mephistopheles.

Federici had risen to stardom in Britain and America in the Savoy Operas of Gilbert and Sullivan, playing the Mikado, the Pirate King, Sir Marmaduke Pointdextre and various other wacky characters of renown. To have him gracing the stages of Melbourne was an honour for the locals, and hopes were high that with his melodious bellow ringing out each night, this run of *Faust* would be a long and profitable one.

At the conclusion of the opera, the characters of Faust and Mephistopheles descend into hell, an effect achieved theatrically by having the actors sink down through a trapdoor on stage. On this opening night, with the final note sung by Federici still echoing in the audience's ears, this was indeed accomplished successfully: both Federici and Leumane descended with a flourish to their fiery fate. The crowd rose

---

* Born Anatole Frederick Demidoff Baker, which seems a fancy enough name for anyone, so why he changed it we cannot surmise.

to applaud enthusiastically, unaware of what was going on below stage.

For as the platform was lowered, Federici suddenly swayed, clutched at Leumane and then fell to the floor, bringing his co-star down with him. While the ovation continued above, stagehands rushed frantically to fetch a doctor. Federici was taken backstage to the green room, where attempts to revive him failed. He had suffered a fatal heart attack. The great singer had belted out his last aria, and at only thirty-seven years old.

It was a terrible tragedy, and brought a period of deep mourning in the southern capital. But beside the tragedy sat a mystery of deep and intoxicating proportions. For while Federici was in the green room, failing to regain consciousness, his fellow cast members were on stage, taking their curtain call. And afterwards, they swore that *Federici had been with them*.

What to say of a man who is dying backstage even while he's taking a bow on stage? It could've been written off as an error on the part of the cast, confused amid the uproar of a successful opening night. It could've been … were it not for the stories that began to emerge from the Princess Theatre in the years after Federici's death.

Stories of lights flashing on and off during performances. Tales of someone brushing past stagehands in empty corridors. And most of all, sightings of a tall, well-dressed man of striking familiarity turning up at the theatre to watch a show.

Yes, Frederick Federici wasn't just determined to take his bow and soak up the applause even after dying: he also refused to allow his untimely departure to keep him from the joys of the opera.

Over the years, many staff and audience members have seen Federici, his fine Italian features, impeccable if old-fashioned haircut and elegant evening dress making him stand out among crowds of theatregoers who, however refined and elite they may be, are not in any way the ghosts of 19th-century singers. Normally, he appears at night and takes a seat in the dress circle, usually in the middle of the second or third row. He's been seen writing notes on the production, and frowning in displeasure at any performances that he deems fall short of his exacting standards. When he's had enough, he drifts down the stairs behind the Royal Box and away into the night.

Federici may haunt the Princess Theatre, but there has never been a hint of anything malevolent about his appearances there. He simply wishes to make his presence known, and to indulge in his love of the theatre, as he did in life. His affection for Melbourne is clear: why else would he stick around to keep a critical eye on the arts scene there? And the affection is reciprocated: for over a century there has been a tradition of keeping a seat in the third row of the dress circle vacant on every opening night, for the use of the theatre's longest-standing patron.

So the story goes, anyway. Is it true? To quote the final line of Mephistopheles in Gounod's *Faust*, 'It might be.'

Sarah

Kapunda, South Australia

If you go to the North Kapunda Hotel, either for a drink or a goggle at the seemingly endless parade of ghosts and ghouls that constantly prance through it, you may want to test your nerve fully with a wander down the 'Hallway to Hell', where long-dead cutthroats roam. Or you could pop down to the cellar, where stacks of corpses were once stored in a makeshift morgue, made necessary by what was an unusually high body count for a pub, even in the 1800s.

Or, for a more peaceful yet sadder communion with the departed, you could head upstairs to Sarah's bedroom. There you will see Sarah's empty bed, her dresses laid out on it, ready to be worn. A rag doll is propped up against the pillow, while a framed drawing of a dapper bear in a straw hat sits on the bedside table. It is a beautifully preserved example of a young girl's bedroom from the 19th century – but the absence of its former inhabitant hangs heavily over it, an oppressive emptiness bearing down on anyone who enters the room.

Sarah is not exactly absent, though. Many have seen her walking around the hotel, silently stalking the floors without ever hinting at who she is or where she came from. Some say she was pushed over the hotel's balcony, killed by the fall. Others claim she was actually the daughter of someone who was murdered in the hotel. Maybe it was the Man in Black who did her – or her parent – in. Certainly, Sarah is now one of the female ghosts resident in the pub whose afterlife is made deeply unpleasant by that spook's attentions.

Sarah is, of course, far from the only North Kapunda-ite to have come to an unfortunate end in the grand old pub. To this day, some visitors encounter the ghost of Hue, a miner who had his leg amputated in one of the hotel's rooms but didn't make it through the procedure. Others have met the ghost of the Aboriginal man who once broke a window in the pub – and was punished for this crime with murder. Ah yes, there is plenty of blood dripping from the North Kapunda Hotel's biography.

But Sarah is something else, something apart. She is just a child, surely no more than eight or nine years old, and her apparition is one that inspires less horror or trepidation and more sadness. Sorrow for a life ended so soon, for a child doomed to wander this pub's floors forever in search of god knows what – her parents? Her killer? Her rag doll? The air is cold where Sarah walks, like a midwinter day when sunshine seems a forlorn hope.

Ghosts are always mysteries, but some are more mysterious than others. With some, it is easy to at least devise a plausible reason for why they might be hanging around here on Earth, refusing to disappear fully into the next world. With others, their presence confounds easy explanation, but nevertheless stands as a bleak reminder of how fragile and ephemeral is life. Sarah has now been wandering the halls in death for many more years than she did in her mortal form, and anyone who stands in her bedroom can feel the pain of the brevity of her life.

Perhaps Sarah's purpose in her ghostly activities is nothing to do with her own story. Perhaps she is there simply to remind us: life is short, eternity is long and the loss of a child is forever worth shedding a tear over.

The New Farm Nightmare

New Farm, Queensland

Nell Brennan was twenty-eight years old when she died. Reuben Wallace was sixty-eight when he was charged, and acquitted, of her manslaughter. And so it was that nobody would ever truly know what happened to Nell – except for Reuben, and Nell herself.

It was 1949, and Reuben Wallace ran the small shop on the corner of James and Robertson streets in New Farm, near the bend in the Brisbane River. Upstairs from the shop was a humble little flat, in which Nell Brennan, before she died, probably regretted ever setting foot. It was in that flat, one dreadful night, that someone or something cut off Nell's oxygen, and the young woman suffocated.

The police said Reuben did it. Reuben pleaded innocence, and in the end he convinced enough members of a jury to ensure that he went free. What really happened in the room above the shop was never discovered. If Reuben Wallace was guilty, he took the secret to his grave. So did Nell.

But spirits are never so restless as when their own demise is veiled in mystery, and as the years went by, and new people moved into the little shop and used it for new purposes, Nell could never quite bring herself to leave.

In 1976, the then residents saw her in the bedroom, lying on the bed, crying out. 'Reuby,' she wailed. 'Reuby!' Reuby was nowhere to be seen, at least not by the eyes of the living. But Nell lay there, calling for him, helplessly, until gradually her form faded from view and the flat fell silent.

Eight years after Nell had first appeared and cried out for Reuby, the occupant of the shop was struck dumb with terror one night when they looked up the stairway to see a woman standing on the landing. A short woman, as Nell Brennan had been, who was looking down the stairs. She was glowing like a lantern in the darkness, emanating a bright white light. This time Nell said nothing, casting her light briefly before vanishing.

Jasmyn Daniels was twenty-eight years old, just like Nell Brennan, in 2009, some twenty-five years after the last reported sighting of Nell. The little shop had by now become a real-estate office, and Jasmyn was working late when she glanced up towards those infamous stairs. At the top of them, outlined starkly against the white wall, she saw the shadow. A woman's silhouette, still and chilling. Jasmyn did not wait to see whether the figure was going to move. 'I couldn't look back up the stairs – I couldn't get out of there fast enough.' Twice more Jasmyn saw the shadow upstairs. Twice more she fled, before deciding to give up staying till late at work.

Today the office is no longer there, but the building remains, and within it the room where Nell Brennan gasped her last breath. It is surely only a matter of time before someone else sees something frightening at the top of those stairs, or hears the plaintive cry of a young woman calling for help. Pleading for Reuby.

The Watchful Widow

Port Stephens, New South Wales

In 2015, volunteers engaged in the renovation of Tomago House, the only National Trust property in Port Stephens, became aware that someone was overseeing their efforts to restore the grand old sandstone pile to its former splendour. After suffering extensive damage during storms that April, the place was in urgent need of rejuvenation, and the Friends of Tomago House were happy to live up to their organisation's name and pitch in. It wasn't long before they discovered that the building had one more friend than they'd first thought.

Tomago House had been constructed in the 1840s by Richard Windeyer, one of Sydney's leading barristers* and a state MP. He had acquired a vast estate of 30,000 acres in the Hunter Valley, and he made the house the centrepiece of this sprawling property. Surrounded by 30 acres of vineyards and fields full of cattle, horses, pigs, sugarcane and wheat, it was a testament to the spectacular success that Windeyer had achieved in the colony since arriving from England in 1835.

Having thus built his empire, and with Tomago House almost ready for him to move into, Windeyer promptly lost all his money, went to Launceston and died.

As well as being a bit of a shock to the Windeyer family, this left

---

* Windeyer's most celebrated case was the Myall Creek Massacre trial, in which he defended those accused of the murders. But, to his credit, he lost.

his widow, Maria, with the job of refinancing the property, completing the outstanding work on it and maintaining its grandeur; tasks which she accomplished with canny efficiency. Maria was what they called in those days 'a force to be reckoned with', and what they call nowadays ... the same thing, really.

Tomago House became Maria's life's work. She did her own housework to save money – which nowadays is no big deal, but back then was tantamount to being a poor person – and made money selling beef and wine, even winning awards for the wine from Tomago's vineyard. In 1860, she added a chapel to the house, because she was a bit weird like that. All in all, she did a magnificent job both in keeping hold of Tomago House despite the debts her husband had left her with, and in retaining its status as a landmark of the Hunter. In 1878, Maria passed away aged eighty-three, no doubt well satisfied with the job she'd done.

In fact, so well satisfied was she that she didn't feel comfortable simply leaving the maintenance of the house for others to carry out unsupervised. And this was what the Friends of Tomago House discovered when they set to work after the storms of 2015: Maria Windeyer, the grand dame of Tomago, was keeping a close eye on them.

They were not the first to notice this, of course. Anyone who went to Tomago House after 1878 could feel Maria's presence there, making sure everything was in order. Down in the cellar, where her prized wines were stored, she has been seen, carefully watching all that goes on. Up on the broad verandah, looking out on the rolling Hunter Valley farmlands, many have reported seeing an old lady in a rocking chair, sitting peacefully, rocking back and forth, and surveying the property that she saved and made great.

The volunteers, eagerly working to ensure the house would continue to dominate the landscape for many years to come, were just the latest in a long line of visitors to encounter the widow Windeyer, and to feel the responsibility of taking good care of her home. No doubt the ghost of Maria breathed a sigh of relief – or whatever ghosts do to indicate relief, since presumably they don't breathe – when the Friends showed up, as she must have feared the storms might ruin Tomago permanently.

But of course she need not have worried. One way or another, as long as Maria Windeyer watches over it, Tomago House will endure, and all who enter it will feel slightly nervous about touching anything.

The Ghost of Glengallan Gate

Glengallan, Queensland

Say it out loud. Just to yourself. 'The Ghost of Glengallan Gate.' Doesn't that sound awesome? You really feel that you're about to be subjected to something incredibly eerie and spooky and wreathed in ominous mists. Perhaps disembodied voices will deliver portentous warnings and heads will float around ballrooms. Is that what will happen, when we hear the tale of … the Ghost of Glengallan Gate? Well, let's see.

It was late on a dark, still night when stockman Daniel Hartigan began the ride back to Goomburra, on the Darling Downs. He was returning from Glengallan and as usual had a skinful of rum to bring with him. At the boundary gate on the road from Glengallan to Goomburra, Hartigan began what was, in his inebriated condition, the arduous task of dismounting his horse in order to open the gate.

It was at this moment that he felt something pushing past him: a shadowy shape that fluttered like a giant moth trying to get ahead in a supermarket queue. At the same time, the Glengallan gate swung open, apparently of its own accord, and Hartigan's horse reared in terror, turned tail and bolted back the way it had come.

Daniel, who had been halfway through the dismounting process, hung on for dear life as the terrified horse skittered along the road, and he scrambled to get back in control and rein the beast in. Turning around, he returned – slowly – to the gate, which was closed once more. Walking the shuddering horse, Hartigan steeled every nerve in his petrified body, nudged the gate open, jumped aboard his steed again and spurred it home as if the legions of hell were on his tail.

Glancing back as he galloped away, he saw the shadow drifting in the trees by the gate.

Back at Goomburra, Daniel Hartigan surprised his colleagues by not being stinking drunk as he usually was after visiting Glengallan. In fact, the second that gate swung open, Hartigan had been rendered stone-cold sober – instead of boisterous intoxication there was only sweaty, shivering panic.

It would be easy to dismiss the anecdote of a drunken stockman – though if we discount every story told by a heavy drinker, a hell of a lot of ghosts don't make the cut. In any case, Daniel Hartigan's is not the only account we have to rely on here. Many other riders, passing through the Glengallan gate, had seen something fluttering in the dark as the gate opened with nobody touching it. Even on the calmest night, when the leaves in the trees hung limp and no wind ruffled the mane of the rider's horse, the gate would still swing open.

Perhaps the most frightening experience of all was that of William Robey, who was riding towards the gate when a ghostly figure rose from the top rail and flew towards him. Robey's horse was so scared that it turned and galloped straight into a tree, which, with the best will in the world, does seem to indicate that it wasn't the smartest horse around. Robey was knocked out, but when he awoke he saw the ghostly figure watching him from the gate. Suddenly it rose once more and floated towards him. In the moonlight, Robey saw that it was nothing but a ghastly head and waving arms. Behind it, the gate swung open.

Eerie, no? Spooky, yes? Probably wreathed in ominous mists, you agree?

Of course, there are those who say that the dread figure Robey saw, and the shadow that fluttered in the trees, was simply a large white owl that used to perch on the gate, and that when it took off it pushed on the top rail and caused the gate to open. This is why, today, at the site of the Glengallan gate there is a sculpture of that white owl, with wings outstretched.

But could it really have been just a bird, all those times that riders in the night saw the shadow, felt it flutter by them and witnessed the gate open and close without a touch? I think I speak for everyone when I suggest: let's say no. The Ghost of Glengallan Gate is much, much more satisfying.

The Martinet Major at Monaro

Monaro, New South Wales

The major, so they said, was a holy terror. Convicts in colonial Australia were not, of course, well treated as a rule, but there was mistreatment and mistreatment, and the major abused his charges as though he was trying to win some kind of contest. Slaving away in the shadows of the Snowy Mountains, the convicts of Monaro were so badly treated that they might as well have been in Tasmania.

Floggings were de rigueur, every man on the chain gang bearing the angry scars of the overseer's whip. If it wasn't the whip, it would be fists and boots and the butts of rifles: cracking skulls and smashing bones. The slightest indiscretion would see the major rain hellfire down on the prisoners: denying them rations, locking them up for days at a time without food or water, setting the dogs on them if he was in the mood for entertainment.

The convicts lived in a permanent state of fear, but also in an equally permanent state of resentment. The major should have known that eventually someone would get sick enough of the abuse to fight back. Then again, maybe he did know and he thought it was worth the occasional bit of pushback to be able to give full rein to his sadism. In fact, he may have welcomed what happened, as it allowed him easy justification for even harsher punishment. Though he clearly didn't foresee the longer-term consequences.

For one of the convicts did indeed reach the end of his rope, and he did indeed decide that something had to be done. It was a futile exercise, of course, for the major had soldiers and guns and the terrible apparatus of the British Empire behind him, while this convict only had a bunch of cellmates who developed a sudden and intense interest in their own feet once the ruckus started.

But even a futile blow for justice is nevertheless a blow for justice, and the brave man made his stand. The only weapon available to the convicts was the stones to be found by the roadside, and so he gathered up a handful and, when the major came by on his horse to inspect the workmen, the prisoner stood and hurled them with all his might.

The major, unhurt by the flurry of stones but outraged at the filthy scum's temerity, saw a great opportunity for his favourite game: String Up the Peasant. Within hours of the first stone pinging against the major's hat, the man who threw it was swinging from a rope. The example had been made, and made well. The rebellion was squashed.

But the major's troubles were just beginning. Not long after the hanging, there began to be heard in the colony the sound of bells ringing in the middle of the night. No culprit could be found, but when everyone had searched in vain for the source of the noise, given up and returned to bed, it would invariably start up again. The major became tired and cranky, and the quality of his savagery really started to suffer.

After a few nights of the bells, the major was woken by a terrible uproar. The cattle in the nearby yard had been released and were romping about the hills. The major was enraged: in his eyes, cows had even less right to freedom than convicts. He and his men were up all night rounding them up again, and the guards were falling asleep leaning on their rifles all the next day.

These were mysterious happenings, but the major only truly got the message when he started getting visits in the night from the man whose neck he'd ordered be-noosed. He was a little bit different from the last time the major saw him: more transparent, emitting a soft glow and in a much better mood. In fact, he was positively boisterous: he would appear late at night at the foot of the major's bed, smiling broadly and singing various popular but extremely rude songs of the period.

The major was shocked and appalled. It was bad enough that he was being tormented by the undead soul of the man he had wronged, but his martinet's heart protested vigorously at being forced to listen to such filthy lyrics at all hours. It was intolerable, and indeed the major did not long tolerate it: after a few nights of raucously profane hauntings, not to mention the continued bell-ringing, he gave in and returned home to England.

And so the convicts of the Monaro, while not actually set free, were at least relieved of the excessive cruelty of their erstwhile tyrant – while the stone-thrower, though paying a considerable price for his rebellion, managed to hang around long enough to call it a win.

The Englishman of Gerringong

Gerringong, New South Wales

It was a dark night and the rain was pattering on the roof of the Gum Tree Inn at Kiama, when the burly sawyers of the Illawarra timberlands looked up from their drinks at the brash young man who had just burst in.

An Englishman he was, newly arrived and set to start work at the Coolangatta property just south of there. A hefty sheepdog shuffled alongside, as his master greeted the locals cheerfully.

'Good evening, gentlemen!' he chirruped. 'Have a drink, all of you! The drinks are on me!'

Every man in the pub roared his approval and moved swiftly to take the newcomer up on his offer, even while they all knew the utter stupidity of what he had just done. Shouting drinks for the whole pub meant that here was a man of some means, and he had walked blithely into a room full of men to whom a pocket full of gold was as blood in the water to a great white.

A couple of hours later, the young man was thoroughly drunk and had made many new friends. Two of them in particular showed great concern for his welfare as he made to leave for home.

'Look here, new chum,' said one of the pair. 'Me and me mate wouldn't dream of letting you walk home alone on such a black night as this. You'd never find your way. We're going south and you're going south – let us guide you.'

The Englishman happily agreed. The three men and the sheepdog left the inn. And never came back.

A few months after the little troupe had vanished into the darkness, a convict became lost in the woods near Gerringong. For four days he stayed in the bush before being found, and to his rescuers he had a hideous tale to tell.

Having lost his bearings while walking in the forest, and with night bearing down, the man made a makeshift shelter out of branches and went to sleep. Awakened by distant thunder, he rolled over and froze in horror. For lying just a few yards away was a crumpled corpse, staring horribly at him with empty eyes, blood running freely down its face. Somewhere in the distance he heard the echoes of an agonised scream, and the sound of sawing.

By the side of the body sat a forlorn-looking sheepdog, whimpering and licking the blood from the terrible wound in the dead man's head.

As he gazed in nightmarish fascination, the sawing noise became louder in his ears. Looking around for the source, he spotted two men, standing over a sawpit, sawing a log.

Now, the man knew, without any doubt, that there had been no sawpit before, nor any men. And who goes out to saw logs in the middle of the night anyway? But they stood before him, sawing away, paying him no mind at all. As the thunder rolled, the convict heard the two men speaking.

'He's still got fifty sovereigns left,' said one. 'That's twenty-five apiece. A nice little nest egg! Now we toss the swine into the fire. And the dog … we must cut its throat.'

The lost convict felt terror rise up in his throat, when suddenly lightning flashed and the whole scene disappeared. But the sight of that awful, mutilated face, those staring dead eyes … that would never leave him. When he was found, he told the whole story.

Though the tale, unsurprisingly, struck some as the ravings of a man suffering from delirium, a search party did set out the day after the rescue to explore the spot where the convict had been found. Nearby they discovered the bones of a man, burned black, and the remains of a dog with knife marks on its throat. They had been killed months ago.

It was years later, in the 1830s, that a man by the name of Jem Hicks walked into the Gum Tree Inn at Kiama, his face pale and haggard as if weathered by years of torment.

As he walked haltingly to the bar, a fellow drinker hailed him. 'Why, Jem, I haven't seen you for years! Last time I saw you was that night the new chum shouted the whole pub. Never saw him again neither!'

Hicks turned towards him with a ghastly visage. Outside, thunder crashed. A dog howled. 'Curse the money!' Hicks wailed wretchedly, pulling at his hair and shaking all over. 'Curse the dog! Am I never to find peace?' With that he staggered desperately from the bar, out the door and into the night, never to be seen again.

Never to be seen ... but those who stumble into a certain glen near Gerringong have still told of witnessing a hellish tableau: two men, sawing at a log, and a dog, mournfully sitting beside his master, as the blood flows freely into the dirt ...

The Visitor at Graham's Castle

Prospect, South Australia

When Prospect House– known locally as 'Graham's Castle' after the man who built it, JB Graham, and its spectacular Gothic Revival style – was demolished at the turn of the 20th century, it was discovered that there were dozens of snakes living in the walls. Many people believed that this rather unsettling revelation explained the eerie experiences reported by people who had lived there. Which could be true, but there are explanations and there are explanations: perhaps the movements of the snakes in the walls accounted for much of the odd sounds and disturbing atmosphere within the castle. Or perhaps the more obvious theory was correct: the snakes were confirmation of the fact that the house had been built on top of a portal to hell.

Maybe that sounds fanciful, but come back to me after thirty or forty snakes have come slithering out of your walls and tell me you're not standing at the entrance to the Eternal Halls of Evil.

The funny thing is that, compared to the mass of serpents that were just inches away from the house's residents at all times, the haunting of Graham's Castle seems almost quaint. Certainly the elegant lady who visited the estate seeking something she never seemed to find did not come across as an aggressive spirit. Curious, and perhaps a little frustrated, but not hostile. But where she came from, and what she was searching for … it's the speculation that so often freezes the blood.

John Benjamin Graham had built his castle in the 1840s, in the Adelaide suburb of Prospect, as a demonstration to all his neighbours that he was really frigging rich. He had made his money by buying shares in a mining company, which is a bit of a cheat, really: that probably explains why he felt so insecure that he had to build a castle.

Prospect House was a marvellous architectural confection, with a crenellated parapet, chimneys and balconies giving it its popular name. Inside were thirty rooms shining with oak and cedar and marble, fitting in well with the general theme the mansion embodied: 'Get a load of ME!'

But from the very beginning, it was not a comfortable place to be. Visitors heard noises at night. There were rustlings in the walls (okay, very likely snakes) and footsteps on the stairs where nobody trod (very unlikely to be snakes). But maybe mysterious noises could be shrugged off if it weren't for the lady.

It began with the sound of a carriage. Nobody ever saw it, but the sound of clip-clopping hooves and rattling wheels was clear as it rolled up the drive. Though the carriage remained invisible, its passenger did not. A lovely, elegant woman, clad from head to toe in finest white silk, would glide gracefully up the house.

She would not go to the door, but instead walk from window to window, peering in as if looking for someone and trying to find out which room they were in. Paying no attention to any residents or staff who might be nearby gaping at the apparition, the lady would vanish after peeking in at a few windows, either returning to whence she came or spiriting herself inside to make the stairs and the floorboards creak under her dainty phantasmic feet.

Night after night, and for many years, the woman would come back to make her investigations. The disturbing sights and sounds of the haunting made sure nobody ever stayed there long. JB Graham himself returned to England, leaving the castle in the care of his stepfather, who sold it a few years later. It passed through numerous hands, with every owner discovering in short order that they'd really rather not have the hassle. In the end, the property was let out to a milkman, who stayed one night and refused to be there any longer.

Eventually, the whole pile was brought crashing down, whereupon those snakes burst free. Hopefully the lady in white finally found what she was looking for.

The Coogee Virgin

Coogee, New South Wales

The pressing question is: does an apparition of the Virgin Mary count as a ghost? Some might argue that when Mary appears, it's more a symbolic transmission from the heavenly realm: more like God's own Bat-Signal than an actual ghost per se.

But within the covers of this book, we have come down on the other side of the argument: the Virgin Mary is dead, and she pops up to give people a bit of a shock; that counts as a ghost as far as we are concerned. If people are going to go around socialising after they die, they don't get out of being called ghosts just because they're Catholic.

Not that we propose to include every appearance of the Virgin in the book: that would make it very monotonous.* But there is at least one persistent holy apparition that merits more attention than the odd bit of toast or coffee foam. This is the legend of the Coogee Virgin, a 21st-century manifestation of the supernatural that also comes with the bracing smell of sea air.

The Virgin first appeared in 2003, when, from the front window of a nearby house, a local man saw something that he described as 'a bit weird'. As he looked out from the aforementioned window, at the small park that overlooked Coogee Beach, he was gobsmacked to see the Virgin Mary – or if not the Virgin Mary, then someone doing an

---

* Though much easier to write, so don't think I didn't consider it.

excellent impression of her – standing by the fence.

Excited by his discovery, he called family and friends around to have a squiz at the Holy Mother as she stood silently on the headland, the ocean a vast blue backdrop behind her. News spread, as it tends to, fast, and the following day there were hundreds amassed at the park to see the Virgin. Given that this was the 21st century, and it was also Coogee – an area of Sydney better known for surfers, backpackers and binge drinkers – seeing such a sacred figure appear was quite a turn-up, although God could be expected to send his messengers where they are most needed.

It wasn't long before thousands of people were coming to Coogee every day to see the Blessed Virgin, who appeared to the faithful between 3.30 and 5pm every afternoon. Pilgrims travelled to the holy fence post to touch and kiss it, and to leave offerings of flowers and rosary beads. And everyone who did so was in agreement: when you looked at the fence, you could definitely see a veiled figure in white standing by the end of it.

There were those who sought to deny the miracle of the Coogee headland. They claimed that what people were seeing was not the Virgin Mary, but simply the way the fence bent at an angle up a small slope in the park, combined with the shadow in late afternoon that made it look like a hooded figure. Up close, the sceptics contended, it was clear that the apparition was nothing but ordinary painted wood.

This was, of course, one possible explanation, but the consensus was that it was the most spoilsporty one. And did we not have to consider the views of the Sydney Archdiocese, which put out an official statement to the effect that they had no idea what it was, but if people wanted to think it was Mary, that was cool with them? Hard to argue with that, isn't it?

Sadly, the Coogee Virgin was not to be a long-lasting miracle. Ten days after she was first sighted, the fence was destroyed by vandals, which meant either that the optical illusion was now impossible to see, or that Mary thought 'to hell with this' and refused to come back.

Which of these is the truth, we shall never know. But it's nice to think that every now and then, when things are looking dark, the ghost of Jesus's mum is ready to come and stand in a park to grant us comfort in our hour of need.

Poor Elizabeth Scott

Melbourne, Victoria

The eleventh of November is a notable date in Australian history. In 1880, it was the day Ned Kelly died. In 1975, it was the day Gough Whitlam was ejected from the prime ministership. In 1918, the date marked the end of the First World War, a war which was famously won by Australia. A less remembered but no less important 11 November occurred earlier than any of these events: in 1863, on the same gallows at Old Melbourne Gaol that would later see the end of Kelly, the first woman to be executed in Victoria was hanged, the end of a short and desperately sad life.

Elizabeth Scott was only thirteen years old when her mother sold her into marriage with thirty-five-year-old Robert Scott. This was back in the days when girls tended to be married off young to ensure they didn't lose their looks in their late teens. Even in those days, though, thirteen was pushing it a little, and many may have looked askance at the marriage had it not taken place out in the country, where nobody can ever be bothered.*

Robert Scott was not only a middle-aged man happy to take a little girl as a bride, he was also a violent drunkard, and Elizabeth bore the brunt of his temper when he was on the grog – which was pretty much always. For ten years the Scotts ran a pub near Mansfield, in country

---

* I mean it's just so *hot*, you know?

166

Victoria. During that time, Elizabeth, besides working behind the bar, bore five children, only two of whom survived infancy.

After all that, had it turned out that Elizabeth had finally got fed up and put a bullet in her husband's brain, none of us, surely, would have blamed her. But as it happens, even after putting up with a decade of the most savage abuse, starting when she was just a child, Elizabeth wasn't Robert's murderer. She wasn't even in the room when he was killed. But they hanged her anyway.

The shotgun blast that shattered Robert Scott's booze-addled brain in April 1863 was fired by Julian Cross, an employee of the Scotts. With him at the time was David Gedge, a groom from the local staging post. Gedge and Cross attempted to make the murder look like suicide, a plan that was seen through faster than a cellophane Bible. Gedge and Cross were arrested for murder, and Elizabeth along with them, the twenty-three-year-old accused of having masterminded the whole thing in order to clear the way for her to shack up with her lover, Gedge.

Whether Gedge really was her lover, or whether Elizabeth had any involvement in the crime at all, is completely unknown, but her comically buffoonish defence lawyer, an utter spud by the name of George Milner Stephen, made no attempt to push back against the prosecution narrative. Nor did he bring the horrific abuse Scott had inflicted on his wife into evidence, or even put Elizabeth on the stand: the defence's entire case was that Elizabeth Scott 'didn't look like a murderer'.

Given it had already been decided by the Melbourne press that Elizabeth was a scheming adulteress, it's no surprise that after just half an hour the jury brought back a guilty verdict. It was no more of a surprise that the well-known 'hanging judge',* William F Stawell, signally failed to confound preconceptions, sentencing her to hang alongside Gedge and Cross.

Elizabeth Scott and David Gedge may have been lovers who plotted

---

* Quite a misnomer, as he never actually hung: in fact, he used to make *other* people hang. Terrible nickname.

to rid themselves of her troublesome husband. Gedge may have just been a friend doing the young woman a favour in freeing her from the violent tyranny of her marriage. Or Gedge and Cross might've done it for reasons unconnected to Elizabeth, simply wanting Scott dead for their own satisfaction – Robert Scott was hardly the kind of man to bring out the milk of human kindness in another.

Whatever the truth of the matter, the last words of Elizabeth Scott to David Gedge ring down the years with unbearable sadness. Turning to the young man beside her on the gallows, Elizabeth pleaded, 'David, will you not clear me now?'

Before Gedge could reply, the trapdoor opened and it was much, much too late. David Gedge did not come to her defence, any more than her lawyer did at the trial, or her mother when she was just a child.

Since that grim November day, a young woman's voice has been heard to echo around the Old Melbourne Gaol. The spirit of Elizabeth Scott, the gaol's first female victim and perhaps its most tragic, resides there still, calling out to visitors from the other side, pleading for justice, for mercy, for someone to hear her story and believe. She may stay there, within those forbidding stone walls, until the gaol itself crumbles, forever crying out, 'Will you not clear me now?'

The Blue Lady

Port Arthur, Tasmania

Port Arthur is a place haunted by any number of lost souls lamenting their violent ends. The nearby Isle of the Dead contains more than 1500 unmarked graves of convicts who fell victim to the port's brutality. Many came to a nasty end in the bush, having escaped in the justified belief that even the slim chance of survival in the wilderness was preferable to the certainty of agony in the colony. In such a place, the Blue Lady's story is a tragedy of a very different sort.

She appears to visitors to the Port Arthur Historic Site, the former prison at the end of the Earth where the British Empire's most troublesome convicts were sent to have the trouble beaten out of them, and where the torturous horrors suffered by prisoners can be felt in the air and the earth of the place by whoever goes there.

But she is not a convict. She is a lady, a young lady with soft features and sad eyes. She wears a long blue crinoline dress and bonnet, and she appears before you with an air of grief and longing, and stretches out her arms towards you, as if pleading for something. Then she vanishes.

Countless tourists at the site have seen the Blue Lady appear and reach out to them. Many others have spotted her at the back door of the building, looking out over the grounds.

She did not come to Port Arthur by force, but as the wife of an accountant who worked in the penal colony. One of very few women to live there, some would see her as a civilising influence on the rough men surrounding her. When she fell pregnant, it would've been a welcome ray of light in a dark place and time.

But happiness was never in Port Arthur's bones. The Blue Lady never became a mother, dying in childbirth along with her baby. Just two more lost souls to add to those who crowd the air there.

This is why the Blue Lady stays at the site, amid the dozens of ghosts who commemorate the prison's bloodstained history. Carrying a grief too powerful to be ended by death, she will return to the building again and again, seeking her lost baby, reaching out arms to hold the infant but never able to. Looking out from the back door, wondering if any of the people passing through have come to bring her child back to her.

It's said that ghosts remain on the mortal plane in order to deal with unfinished business. But it seems more likely that they remain in order to play out business that can never be finished, again and again for eternity. Like the Blue Lady, the saddest ghost in the saddest place in Australia, who lost her life and her baby at the same time, and won't stop coming back until one or the other is restored.

But they never will be.

Emily and Her Sister

Kapunda, South Australia

Ah, 'tis our old friend, the North Kapunda Hotel, Australia's most haunted pub and a place that is filled with spectral echoes of blood and terror, scary even by South Australian standards. It should be clear by now that this old watering hole is so packed with spooks and spirits that it's a wonder anyone can get to the bar for all the ectoplasm in the way.

The ghosts of the North Kapunda Hotel can be roughly divided into two categories: the angry jerk ghosts who spend their time harassing people, and the timid ghosts who spend their time trying to stay out of the way of the angry jerk ghosts. The former can be found roaming freely about the building, such as in the 'Hallway to Hell', where guests have reported being pushed and screamed at; or in the basement, where once corpses were piled up for reasons that can't be properly understood without a deep knowledge of colonial Australian culture and an extremely disturbing worldview. The latter, meanwhile, can be found in their old rooms upstairs, wishing they were still alive or at least that they could get out of the bloody North Kapunda Hotel.

Emily, the fifteen-year-old girl who lives – in the loosest sense of the word – with her sister upstairs at the North Kapunda is far from the most terrifying ghost you'll meet. In fact, you might want to seek her out for some company if you've had enough of the more robust phantoms in the pub.

Nobody knows where Emily and her sister came from. Presumably they used to live in, or at least regularly visit, the hotel. Perhaps they were friends of Sarah, the poor little girl whose room is still kept immaculate for visitors to see and feel awkward in. Perhaps they were the daughters of a long-forgotten innkeeper, or of a hard-drinking local who would leave them to their own devices while he whiled away the hours at the bar.

You'll see the two girls in one of the rooms upstairs, where Emily sits on the windowsill and looks out on the courtyard. It's said they stay in that room to avoid the attentions of one of the pub's other residents – most likely the Man in Black, who is just the type of obnoxious arse who would go around harassing teenage girls. Of course, once you're a ghost already there's a limited amount of damage that another ghost can do to you, but nevertheless it's probably unpleasant.

And so Emily spends her days gazing at the courtyard and occasionally giving intruders a sort of languid, melancholy scare: the kind of scare where you don't so much jump in fright as sort of let your shoulders sag and let out a sigh. Emily's sister will at the same time look up at you with wide, adorable eyes that are nevertheless creepy in that very special way that ghost kids' eyes always are.

If you're up for it, you could spend a peaceful half an hour sitting with the girls in their room, thinking about life and how awful it is. Emily's gaze always returns to the outdoors, where she yearns to escape but can't, because something, some sinister contract or other, binds her to this cursed hotel. Downstairs, it could be that the ghost of her father is still downing beer after incorporeal beer; upstairs, a sad little oasis has developed, where two young girls who will never grow up keep to themselves and wish with all their hearts that they could be anywhere but there.

The Mushroom Tunnel

Picton, New South Wales

Some places, for whatever reason, are simply more ghost-infested than others. If ghosts were soccer, then places like North Kapunda and Port Arthur would be the Brazil and Argentina of the haunting world. Under this system, Picton, south-west of Sydney, is Germany: maybe not as flamboyant as those others, but always in the mix and getting its hauntings done with ruthless efficiency. Picton has no wish to show off, but in its quiet way it's been filling up with ghosts for centuries, and is quite prepared to spook you from here to breakfast-time if you venture out that way.

It is a great shame that, for those who do head to Picton in search of scares, it is no longer possible to enter the Mushroom Tunnel. For within the Mushroom Tunnel dwell dark and dreadful things, such as could, if not turn your hair bone-white exactly, at least sprinkle a decent helping of icing sugar on it for effect. Sadly, health and safety requirements[*] mean it can now only be viewed from the outside. Still, there's enough creepiness radiating from within to make that worth doing. And of course, as in any situation in life, you always have the option of completely ignoring health and safety requirements. For the ghosts certainly do …

The official name of the Mushroom Tunnel is the Redbank Range

---

[*] When don't they spoil our fun, right?

Railway Tunnel. It was, in fact, the first tunnel used by the New South Wales Railway, in 1867. In 1919 it was closed to rail, and subsequently used to store arms and ammunition during the Second World War, and later to commercially grow mushrooms, hence its popular name. Today the guns and the mushrooms are gone, leaving only a dark and desolate stretch where every sound echoes weirdly off the stonework and your eyes will play tricks on you.

The tunnel itself is in a suitably creepy spot. With the railway long gone and no practical function being performed anymore, it's a looming black mouth amid overgrown foliage, down a gravel track. As you walk towards it, it is hard to quieten the voice in your head screaming that if you go inside, you will never come out.

The tunnel has been a magnet for tragedy. In the days when trains still rushed through it, one unhappy young girl laid herself on the rails and let the wheels crush her. This may be the same girl who some have seen, all in white, wafting in and out of the tunnel. If you listen really closely, you might even hear the faint sound of her voice crying, 'Didn't think that through ...'

Even more regretful is Emily Bollard, who turned out to be far less sturdy than her surname suggested. Emily is often seen right in the middle of the 180-metre tunnel, on the very spot on which she was standing when the train hit her, in 1916, while she was taking what turned out to be a very inefficient short cut. The apparition of the middle-aged woman appears before your eyes with a plaintive look, as if to say, 'No, it's not due for another five minutes.' It's said that she will reach out and touch your hair and body, having very little respect for personal space.

The glowing figures of unfortunate women are not the end of the Mushroom Tunnel's dread wonders. If you dare to get close enough, you will see the black shadows that race up and down its length, as though the tunnel itself is remembering trains gone by. Those who walk down it have seen white lights appear above their heads, and the figures of faceless people flash before their eyes. The sounds of children running and laughing down the tunnel can be heard; some have even caught glimpses of kids trotting in and out of the shadows.

But perhaps most frightening of all – at least for those with a keen sense of self-preservation – are those moments when visitors to the tunnel have felt the air grow suddenly cold and a wind come rushing through the darkness, as if a train is bearing down on you right at that second. For the Mushroom Tunnel never forgets, and all its memories will be waiting for you on the day you summon the courage to come near that lonely black hole.

The Cemetery Children

Picton, New South Wales

Shall we stay a while in Picton, then? Why not, indeed? We have visited the picturesque old maternity hospital, been choked by the jolly old matron and had some disturbing fun in a disused railway tunnel. It's time, then, to really get the party started, with a trip to St Mark's Cemetery.

It was 9 January 2010 when Renee English took a trip to that very cemetery, having heard tales of ghost tours running regularly for a reasonable fee. Ms English swore blind after 'the incident' that she had never previously believed in ghosts – which is fine, but everyone always says that, don't they? Anyway, for what it's worth, yes, she does claim to have been a 'sceptic' when she started taking photos at the cemetery.

'I was just snapping away and making jokes about the whole thing,' says Ms English, and you can imagine the kind of thing. 'This is the dead centre of town', 'people are dying to get in here' and so forth. Little did she know, when she was entertaining her family with these zingers, that her camera had captured something quite un-comedic. On that subject, Ms English was to say: 'I know that when I took that photo, there was no one else in the cemetery.'

The photo in question was a snap of the historically significant graves in St Mark's, with a couple of interesting details: two children, dressed in white, passing by the tombstones in the background. When

Ms English saw the photo she'd taken, in her words, 'all the hairs on my arms stood up and I just went cold all over'. There could be no doubt: she had the flu.

Just kidding! Of course, the reason she went cold and stiff-haired was that, as she'd said, there was no one else in the cemetery, yet her camera had captured the two children wandering amid the stones.

There are plenty, of course, who pooh-pooh the picture.* And it's fiendishly difficult to prove that a photo of ghost children is real, since the difference between a photo of ghost children and a photo of non-ghost children is, in practice, negligible. But Renee English is far from the first person to claim St Mark's Cemetery is haunted, and those who've told the tale before know exactly who it's haunted by.

Blanche Moon was the daughter of Henry and Fanny Moon, the former being a Picton timber worker. In 1886, eleven-year-old Blanche was playing with friends on a pile of railway sleepers when she slipped and fell. The sleepers toppled over, crushing the little girl's leg. She was rushed to hospital and died there.

Sixty years later, David Shaw, son of a local minister, died of polio. He was buried in St Mark's, just like Blanche Moon and her little brother Alfred, who died at the age of two. Alfred and Blanche share a headstone in the graveyard, but it's David who accompanies Blanche on her walks around the grounds – and it's those two who Renee English apparently caught on camera on a hot January day in 2010.

It's a mournful thought: the two kids, taken suddenly and far too soon, leaving behind the rivers of tears in their parents' eyes, walking through the cemetery together, trapped forever among the dead. And it's a mournful place, the Picton cemetery, the supposedly final resting place of generations in a town where it sometimes seems nobody really gets to rest at all.

But there's something sweet and hopeful about the sight of Blanche and David wandering St Mark's together, because that's exactly what they are: together. Being a ghost seems like a lonely lifestyle, and all

---

* Not literally.

the more so for a child. If these two youngsters, taken by tragedy and separated by six decades, have in the afterlife found each other, their friendship might be cause for uplift in that grim and sombre place.

Captain Logan, the Tyrant of Moreton Bay

Moreton Bay, Queensland

The year was 1825, and the Governor of New South Wales, Thomas Brisbane, had a problem: the Moreton Bay Penal Settlement.[*] It was a shambles: nothing but a bunch of tents huddling on the north bank of the Brisbane River,[†] filled with convicts who kept whining about petty concerns like death by starvation. Vexingly for the Governor, Queensland had not been invented yet, so the nasty little colony was his responsibility, and people kept nagging him to do something to make it slightly less of a bottomless pit of human misery. Why they did this, nobody knows – bottomless pits of human misery were the whole point of penal settlements – but the fact remained that Brisbane felt compelled to do something.

Following the old Governors' Maxim – 'when in doubt, get in a real bastard' – Brisbane sent for Captain Patrick Logan, a Scot, to take up the post of commandant at Moreton Bay. Arriving in March 1826, Logan quickly got to work improving the settlement. Introducing radical new innovations such as 'buildings' and 'food', he swiftly turned Moreton Bay from a primitive camp of starving wretches into a thriving town of slightly-better-nourished wretches.

---

[*] Which was at the time located in New South Wales: they didn't move Moreton Bay to Queensland until later.

[†] Named after the Governor himself, and don't think he didn't mention THAT at every party he ever went to.

179

But although the Governor and the establishment of the day thanked Logan for his efforts, the same could not be said of the convict population of Moreton Bay, who rather short-sightedly ignored the construction of the hospital and the windmill, and focused obsessively on the captain's relentless brutality. Logan rapidly became known for his disciplinary philosophy, which could be summed up as 'keep whipping them until they shut up'. The convicts, unappreciative of motivational techniques that left their backs riddled with scars, dubbed Logan 'the Fell Tyrant' for his abusive nature and lack of equilibrium.

It was while returning to the settlement from an expedition one night, alone on horseback, that Captain Logan had his first foreshadowing of the reckoning that fate had in store for him. For near a patch of woods, he caught sight of a lone convict and, assuming him to be attempting an escape, called out to him to, in so many words, 'get the hell over here'.

The absconder, to Logan's surprise, obeyed without demur. In fact, he strode purposefully over to the captain's horse. As he approached, Logan saw clearly the dreadful look upon his face: great staring eyes fixed upon him with a deathly gaze. When he reached the horse's side, the man suddenly grabbed hold of Logan's stirrup.

The captain, startled by this unprecedented act of impudence, immediately brought his hunting crop down on the cheeky fellow. It was then that Logan noticed something odd: instead of the crop striking the man, as had always been the case in the past when doling out a thrashing, it went straight through him. Indeed, as he attempted to rain blows upon his assailant, the crop instead struck hard on the flank of his horse, causing the animal not a little agitation.

So there was Captain Logan, struggling to keep control of his horse as it reared and bucked with alarm at the unexpected flogging it was receiving, while also trying to stay in the saddle in spite of the grim-faced attacker yanking at his stirrup. He seemed just about to go apex over nadir, when, with a suddenness that those familiar with the laws of physics might've found alarming, the convict was gone. Not a trace of him anywhere, and the captain was once again alone with his horse.

It was a disturbing experience for the captain, made even more disturbing by the fact that he had recognised the wide-eyed apparition. It was Stimson, a convict who had recently died at Moreton Bay after one of Logan's patented lashings. This was enough to make a man think.

If the revenge of dead convicts was blood-chilling, it was nothing compared to the revenge of living ones. Not long after the midnight encounter with Stimson's phantom, Logan – apparently having failed to learn his lesson – was again riding alone through the countryside when he was ambushed by a pack of his penal charges. Expressing their grievances to management in a forthright – some might even say blunt – manner, the convicts proceeded to terminate Logan's tenure as commandant with extreme finality.

The death of Logan, as you'd expect, put a stop to the mistreatment of marginalised people in Australia forever,[*] but it wasn't the end of his story. Taking inspiration from the spooky stirrup-grabber, the Fell Tyrant[†] continued to make his presence felt around Moreton Bay.

The first sighting of Logan's ghost occurred just after he had died – in fact, before he'd even been reported missing. Convicts working on the north bank of the Brisbane River saw Logan on his horse on the south bank, signalling to them to row him across. By the time they got to him, he'd disappeared, which was rude but totally in character.

After that Logan appeared frequently: in Ipswich, by the Logan River and in the Brisbane River Valley. He rides around his old haunts restlessly, seeking out underlings to berate and prisoners to abuse, doomed to eternal frustration as, in incorporeal form, he can't flog anybody. Perhaps in death he has met up again with Stimson and talked over their differences. It would be nice to think that enemies,

---

[*]   Citation needed.

[†]   The sobriquet 'The Fell Tyrant' was given to Logan by convict William Ross, who wrote a novel with that title based on his experiences with the tender mercies of Logan and the colonial penal system. It should not be confused with a 'tyrant who fell', although Logan turned out to be one of those too, in the end.

once united in ghosthood, could become friends. Alas, it's more likely that the Fell Tyrant of Moreton Bay is still swinging his hunting crop at all and sundry, to no avail.

Hats Off to Her

Brisbane, Queensland

The Brisbane Arcade is, we already know, an excellent spot to find ghosts. It's a lovely retro building, opened in 1924 but built in a style harking back further, to the Victorian era, with broad balconies, iron balustrades and huge high windows. Strolling through the arcade, one finds a charming array of shops both quaint and tastefully expensive. The point is, it's a place whose vibe can be truthfully described as 'old-timey', which as usual means plenty of spooky stuff to be revealed.

You see, there once was a lady, and that lady had a shop on the gallery level of the Brisbane Arcade. In this shop she sold hats of her own making, and charged prices as extravagant as the designs. For a woman of Brisbane society wishing to make an impression at a function, or to look more ridiculous than her friends at the races, the arcade was the place to go, where the gallery milliner would outfit your head in the most fabulous and excessive manner.

The lady herself, though devoted to her life's work of creating fantasias of headwear for the fashion-conscious and cashed up, was not devoid of the commoner human passions either. And why should she be? Should a peculiar talent for the costumerie of the human anatomy's upper portions mean that a woman gives up hopes of love? Surely not, and certainly not in the case of the milliner, who, as it happened, fell in love, and fell hard.

But just as a gauzy fascinator is no guarantee of winning Fashions on the Field, falling in love is no guarantee of happiness. The romance that our lady threw herself into with gusto did not end with happily ever after: instead, the chap in question called it quits and the milliner was left alone and heartbroken.

The end of a love affair can be a devastating thing. All colour drains from the world, life becomes devoid of anything to savour. Once the object of her grand passion, hats suddenly seemed the most trivial and futile of garments. What point was there in adorning the head, she wondered, when the heart lay in ruins? It's a question we might all ponder, although those of us who do not make hats might find it somewhat tangential to our own experience.

For the milliner of the gallery, there was now no denying that hats were but a particularly pointless part of that colossal waste of time known as life. Without love, what purpose could life even have, she asked herself, and in answer came up empty. So it was that one lonely night, the lady stood upon the balcony in the Brisbane Arcade, looked down at the shining marble floor below and, with a tear trickling down her cheek, threw herself from the gallery level to the ground, where her neck was broken and her broken heart stopped. As I said: she fell in love, and fell hard.

Thus ended the unhappy life of the milliner of the Brisbane Arcade, but thus did not end her story. For though in the throes of heartbreak she may have sworn off her life's work, in death she seemingly discovered some perspective. It can happen. She willingly quit the world of the living, but then found that she could not bring herself to quit her business. For along the walkways of the gallery she promenades even today, striding with purpose past her shop and others, keeping a watchful eye on the temple of retail that once counted her among its most enthusiastic merchants.

You may see her in the arcade, looking down over the balconies and examining the window displays. She pays no heed to passers-by or gawkers: she has more important business. She is dressed, as one might imagine, all in black, though on her head she sports something a little extra, only fitting for such a lady. A marvellous construction it is: broad and high and embellished with cream lace. It is a mourning bonnet, but one gorgeous enough to leave no one in any doubt that here walks the milliner of the gallery, and her splendour is undiminished.

Join the Club

Picton, New South Wales

Henry Colden Antill was born in New York, the son of John Antill, who fought for the British in the American War of Independence and was forced to take his family to Canada after realising just how wrong a horse he had backed. Young Henry also joined the British Army, suffering a very glamorous wound in India and eventually pitching up in New South Wales with his friend Governor Lachlan Macquarie.

Once in the colony, Major Antill was given a grant of land, naming his new property Jarvisfield, after the governor's first wife's maiden name – which seems a rather convoluted way to name something, but these were more formal times. Jarvisfield was located in the area then known as Stonequarry, but having built his estate there, the major renamed the latter Picton.* So you can see where this is going.

Henry Antill probably didn't know, when he settled there and started his family, that he was establishing a ghost-magnet for centuries to come, but it's nice to think he would've approved. He was, after all, quite progressive for the times, being a great supporter of causes such as Aboriginal welfare, orphans' rights and emancipation: there's no reason to think he wouldn't have supported the rights of ghosts as well.

---

* The name Picton was chosen to honour Sir Thomas Picton, who was killed while saving the day at the Battle of Waterloo. To this day, the town takes enormous pride in its hatred of the French.

Antill prospered and multiplied in his time at Picton, and his family was resident at Jarvisfield until the 1930s. Today, Jarvisfield is the site of the Antill Park Golf Club, while overlooking the property is Vault Hill, the cemetery where Major Antill and twelve of his relations are buried. It's said the major was buried standing upright so that he could overlook his estate, which indicates either that Henry Antill just did not understand the basic facts of life, or that he had a belief in life after death that was completely appropriate for the man who founded Picton.

It's down at the golf club, though, where the action is – which is not something you can usually say. The Antills' old homestead is now the clubhouse, and within its walls for many years have been occurring certain … occurrences.

There are particular rooms, regulars say, in which a person will begin to feel ill upon entering them. There is a strange atmosphere that will all of a sudden come over the place, as if a black cloud has appeared overhead. The clubhouse becomes darker, quieter, and a sourness permeates the air, as if the house itself is dropping a hint. Bangs and crashes come from empty rooms, and doors slam without a breath of wind. In the games room, from time to time, the jukebox will, of its own accord, burst into life and start playing music, as if a dance were starting for a gathering of partygoers who can't be seen.

Then there is the old man and the little girl. They've been on the homestead since long before the golf club was established. The old man is a lonely old man, who has kept the girl, about twelve years old, with him for company for nearly two hundred years. They loiter in the clubhouse, longing for the company of people they can't touch or speak to, wishing they could be free of this world but bound to it by god only knows what. Some say they cannot be released until the old Antill house is finally demolished. Others say, 'Oh, you're just making that up.'

Whatever the truth, anyone heading to Picton for a round of golf is unlikely to find it as relaxing as the brochures make it seem. And through it all, Major Henry Colden Antill remains, up on Vault Hill, looking down upon the haunted domain he brought into being.

And His Ghost May Be Heard …

Dagworth Station, Queensland

All countries have ghost stories, but only one has turned a ghost story into its most popular patriotic song.[*] Of course, 'Waltzing Matilda' isn't just a ghost story: it's also a cheerful tale of suicide and, depending on your point of view, an account of either justice or injustice done. It might even be a political protest song. The simple ditty, the words of which were penned by Banjo Paterson in 1895, contains multitudes and, like all the best telemovies, is based on a true story.

The Great Shearers' Strike of 1891 had torn the colony of Queensland apart and seen the army called in, before the strikers were forced by hunger and penury to give in. But the spark of rebellion had been lit, and in 1894 another strike broke out among the shearers at Dagworth Station, in north-west Queensland.

With the situation tense, the owner of Dagworth brought the police in to bring the shearers to heel. In response, the shearers fired their guns in the air and burned down the woolshed, killing dozens of sheep – which was grossly unfair because the sheep hadn't done anything and in all likelihood would've supported the principle of union solidarity, had they been given a chance and had the political ramifications[†] carefully

---

[*]   Unless you consider the Queen of England to be a ghost, and if you do I won't argue.

[†]   *Ram*ifications? Get it?

188

explained to them. Alas, nobody bothered to do so, and the poor woolly wretches were roasted alive.

At the point of the woolshed going up in flames, all hell broke loose. The troopers moved in and the shearers scattered. Into the bush fled one shearer by the name of Samuel Hoffmeister, a Dutch immigrant from Batavia,* who was known around Dagworth as 'Frenchy' because shearers couldn't tell the difference between European accents.

Hoffmeister ran for his life, pursued by three policemen and the owner of Dagworth Station himself. It was 12.30pm on 2 September 1894 when the exhausted shearer reached 4 Mile Creek and, realising that there was no way he was going to escape the chase, drew his gun and shot himself. They never did take him alive.

It's not exactly the same story we all sang about in school. Hoffmeister was no swagman, but a union-strong shearer running from the law. He didn't drown himself in a billabong,† but shot himself. And rather than stuffing a jumbuck in his tuckerbag, he and his friends had burned the jumbucks in their shed. But the core of the tale was there, and it was this story that was told to Banjo Paterson by his friend Bob Macpherson, who lived at Winton, not far from Dagworth.

Paterson was inspired by the story to write down his famous lyrics, which he set to a tune played by Bob's sister Christina, on whom Banjo was quite keen, despite the fact he had a fiancée at the time, the dirty little devil. He called the song 'Waltzing Matilda', which was old outback slang for having sex with a sleeping bag or some weird thing. The rest is history. As indeed was the bit before that. It's all history, in fact.

As for Frenchy Hoffmeister, he was soon forgotten, as were his comrades in the Dagworth Strike of '94, their part in the labour movement becoming as obscure as their part in the creation of Australia's most famous song. There are some who suggest that his

---

* Now Jakarta: Batavia was the capital of the Dutch East Indies, back in the days when the Dutch were far too big for their britches.

† Though very near the place where he shot himself, there is a waterhole dubbed 'Waltzing Matilda Billabong' in honour of the legend. You can find it around twenty kilometres east of Kynuna.

suicide was, in fact, no such thing: that the troopers gunned him down by the creek to show people what happened to workers who talked back to authority.

Impossible to know, now, whether the poor sod was murdered by the coppers or just chased to despair by them. But if you're desperate to discover the truth, you could go and ask him. Head down to 4 Mile Creek, just outside Kynuna, down the road from Dagworth Cemetery.

For there, his ghost may be heard …

Polly McQuinn

Euroa, Victoria

Polly McQuinn was riding back from Euroa, pulling a jinker laden with supplies for the Strathbogie Run. The night was dark and the rain heavy, so a man couldn't see three feet in front of his face. Polly had left it late to return, having lingered in Euroa for more than the odd drink. Even on a dry night with clear skies it would've been a dangerous business riding home in his condition: as it was, Polly and his jinker weaved with artistic flair from one side of the road to the other as the rain lashed man and horse, and the ground turned to slush beneath his steed's hooves. Ahead was Seven Creeks, rising by the minute.

Some say he was named Polly because even in adulthood he could never grow a beard – just like a woman, or a parrot. Others say Polly was simply short for Pollock, and that he was perfectly capable of facial hair. Either way he'd drawn a bad hand nomenclature-wise, which may have explained his drinking problem, but that's not important right now. What is important is that on that fateful night in the rough and ready 1860s, he was full of fine sherry and atop a horse trotting unsteadily through the rainstorm towards the ford at Seven Creeks.

The creek was swollen, the water fast and dark, and the crossing more treacherous than ever. Just downstream from the crossing, the creek formed a pool, a lovely place to swim on a hot summer's day – which this was decidedly not.

Polly was just about managing to stay in the saddle when he came to the crossing. His horse was reluctant to keep going, snorting and whinnying on the muddy bank, attempting to make his rider see reason. But Polly had a home to get to and a bed to sleep off tonight in, and he urged the creature forward. The jinker rattled and clattered behind them as they moved hesitantly into the stream.

The creek was deeper than normal, and the stream racing faster than Polly had ever known it. The horse scrambled for its footing in the rushing water. Its hooves slipped. Polly urged it forward again, hoping to sprint quickly across the ford. But the horse stumbled, the jinker tipped sideways, and suddenly man and horse were both flailing in the current.

Polly never had a chance: the creek was too swollen, his reactions too slow. His horse, with rider tangled and the trailer still hitched up and dragging him down, was equally doomed. Together they were swept down the creek and into the waterhole, where they struggled briefly and in vain. Polly McQuinn and his horse sank beneath the pitch-black waters and were never seen again.

Well, that's not quite true. Though the poor horse was indeed never seen again, Polly himself puts in the occasional appearance. In fact, every seven years, so it's said, he can be seen on a moonlit night, standing by the bridge that now spans the creek, and which would really have come in handy back when he was trying to cross it.

When you can't see Polly, you may still hear him. Drive five minutes down Polly McQuinns Road from Strathbogie, to Polly McQuinn Weir – the very waterhole where Polly was lost, and now a popular holiday spot. There, if you wait till nightfall, you will hear poor old Polly crying out for help, just as he did all those years ago before slipping beneath the inky waters that now bear his name.

The Vengeful Sailor

Sydney, New South Wales

Since 1887, the Russell Hotel has stood on the corner of George Street and Globe Street in the heart of The Rocks, where the bricks and mortar breathe with the bloody, bawdy, booze-soaked history of Old Sydney Town. The place has done service as a sailors' hostel, a brothel and a makeshift plague hospital. Larrikins and cutthroats and dissolute undesirables of all kinds have passed through the hotel's doors, some of them never to come back out – not upright, anyway.

One sailor in particular developed an unusually close bond with the Russell, after stopping there one night in search of a cold drink, a warm bed and whatever further entertainments could be found therein. He was far from the only sailor to frequent the hotel: on any given night, all of Sydney knew that the Russell would be awash with seamen.* That night was a rowdy one: as bellies grew fuller and fuller with rum, the singing got louder, the tales of knife fights with giant squids became more boastful, and the accidental jostling grew more likely to erupt into fisticuffs. It was really just another night in The Rocks, which by the late 1800s had already for a century been the best place to go for a fight and a frolic and to forget what an awful place you lived in.

Yes, the Russell was filled with sailors in varying states of consciousness and alcoholism. But we are concerned with one particular sailor,

---

* BOOM!

because unlike the other mariners who came to the hotel that night, this one would never leave. And all because at some point during the evening, after he'd begun downing the rum but before he'd downed so much that the bar staff could easily pick his pockets, he met a young lady and hit it off something marvellous.

The sailor and the lady were getting on so well, in fact, that the suggestion was later floated that, since the bar was so awfully loud, and since they were enjoying this conversation so much, didn't it make sense that they go somewhere a little quieter, the better to appreciate each other's repartee? The woman mentioned that Room 8, upstairs, would be ideal; the man immediately saw the merits of the proposal.

Up to this point, things were going well. The sailor and his new friend made their way upstairs, and once behind closed doors events proceeded basically upon the lines that both had been anticipating. For the sailor, it was a satisfying bit of shore leave. For the young woman, it was a decent hour's work.

But at some point things went a little off-script. It seems likely that it was a dispute over money, a subject which so often interferes with budding new relationships. It's possible that a philosophical dispute arose with regard to the couple's individual financial ideologies. It's also possible that the lady and the sailor differed widely in their opinion as to what was the optimal destination for the money currently in the room.

Whatever the specifics, the argument quickly became even more heated than the embraces of a few minutes earlier, and the man and woman came to blows. And not in a good way. One might have expected a burly sailor to have an almost ungentlemanly advantage in such a fracas, but this was a lady who ensured, whenever she was at the Russell Hotel, that she was as prepared as any boy scout. No sooner had the sailor advanced on her than she had whipped a blade from her stocking and stuck the brute between his ribs, ensuring his ship would leave harbour down on manpower.

It was a dreadful occurrence, but not at all out of keeping with the Russell's general ambience. But it was after that night that the staff of the hotel began to notice the changes. The creaking floorboards. The heavy feet pacing. The sounds emanating from an empty room: Room 8.

Not just sounds, either: the sailor would occasionally appear, scowling and brooding. But only ever when Room 8 was occupied, and only ever when the occupant was a woman, sleeping alone. At those times he materialises, to watch the guest through the night. Perhaps he is waiting for a particular woman to show up. Perhaps he is hoping that one day he will get the chance to take revenge for his own death. If so, he will likely be waiting a long time, but in the meantime he has put in many years' solid work creeping the hell out of generations.

Lonely Bronia

Brisbane, Queensland

There is surely no arcade in all the world so filled with sadness and tragic memories as the Brisbane Arcade. If you walk through it today, you could probably find a depressing story behind every shopfront, and not just the story of modern capitalism's oppression of the small-business owner. But in all the blood-soaked, tear-stained history of the Brisbane Arcade, is there any tale so melancholy as that of Bronia Armstrong?[*]

Bronia Armstrong was just nineteen years old and worked in the offices of the Brisbane Associated Friendly Societies' Institute[†] above the arcade. She was secretary to Reginald Wingfield Spence Brown, an accountant thirty years her senior, and by strange coincidence she was also dating Brown's son Ian.

Reg Brown was an unprepossessing, mild-mannered, middle-aged man, thinning on top and sporting owlish spectacles. If photographs of him show a slightly unsettling smile and a disconcerting stariness to his eyes, it is possible that our perception is being coloured by what we know of the man. For in 1947, Reg Brown was convicted of the murder of Bronia Armstrong, a crime as stomach-turningly brutal as they come.

The story went that Reg had developed an obsession with his pretty

---

[*]   No. There is not.

[†]   Catchy name, right?

teenage secretary, an obsession perhaps fuelled by jealousy of his son's relationship with her. On 10 January 1947, it is alleged he gave in to his grimmest urges and attacked Bronia Armstrong in the office, when no one else was present. The young woman fought back hard – wounds were found on Brown's hands – and she screamed her lungs out, but the accountant knelt on top of her and pressed down on her chest to suffocate her. Her half-naked body was found in the BAFSI offices the next morning by co-worker Lorna Major. By 6pm that night, Reginald Brown had been charged with her murder.

Although Brown denied any part in the atrocity, and claimed he had been assaulted by two men the day before the murder to explain away his injuries, the jury was having none of it. The judge called it 'one of the most brutal and pathetic cases in the history of Queensland crimes', and sentenced the nerdy accountant to life with hard labour. Nine days into his sentence, Reg Brown hanged himself in his cell, leaving behind a note in which he again proclaimed his innocence.

At the time, Brown's guilt was taken as a given, but in recent years some have cast doubt on the conviction, raising the possibility that he never got a fair trial and Bronia's real killer was never found. The truth may remain a matter of dispute forever, which puts an interesting complexion on the other legacy of the case: the ghost of Bronia Armstrong.

For in the office where Bronia worked, and in which she suffered that terrible fate, her spirit is said to remain. In that little corner of the Brisbane Arcade, objects move about seemingly of their own accord. The electricity goes out without warning. Lights flicker, breezes blow indoors. It does seem that Bronia has stuck around in her old workplace to …

To what? To grieve her own demise? To warn others of the dangers a young girl faces if she trusts a man? Or something perhaps even more upsetting: could Bronia Armstrong continue to haunt the Brisbane Arcade because she knows an injustice has been done, and can't find peace until an innocent man's name is cleared? Three people, at most, knew whether Reg Brown killed Bronia Armstrong: Reg, Bronia and – if he didn't do it – the real murderer. If the lonely spirit of that lively girl is still at work, maybe it's the truth she's waiting for.

You'll Seymour Ghosts at the Royal Hotel

Seymour, Victoria

One hundred kilometres north of Melbourne lies the cheerful town of Seymour, and in the heart of Seymour lies the Royal Hotel, a popular destination over the years for tired and thirsty travellers. Besides its regular functions, since its opening in 1848 the Royal has also acted as a courthouse, a morgue, a post office, a police station and a Cobb & Co. coach stop. It's a venue of infinite versatility, a quality also expressed in the way the hotel offers hospitality with equal generosity to the living and the dead.

The Royal Hotel has always had a close relationship with death, even when not being used as a morgue. It's said that the head of Mad Dan Morgan was displayed proudly on the bar while en route to Melbourne; a replica of Morgan's death mask is still used today in ghost tours, purportedly to kickstart the haunting and give the punters their money's worth. This is, of course, patently ridiculous: firstly, because a replica death mask quite obviously holds no magical power; and secondly, because the Royal Hotel doesn't need any help in providing spectral shenanigans. As a spookhouse, it's absolutely jam-packed with the dearly departed.

You can't swing a cat in the Royal* without having the cat pass eerily straight through a departed soul. If you get the chance to visit, whether

---

* And even if you could, you shouldn't.

on an official ghost tour or not, you're likely to get a decent show. Sit in the bar a while and you may see a glass fly into the air and turn over of its own volition. Wander around the building and you might experience a rising sense of panic as footsteps follow you, with no feet attached.

What on earth *happened* at the Royal Hotel to make the ghost community gather there in such numbers and with such enthusiasm? Well, it would seem the answer is: rather a lot. Specifics are hard to come by, but when your pub is haunted by an entire ghostly band, playing at the end of the ballroom, you've got to assume something truly spectacular took place. A band: that's got a real *Shining* vibe, hasn't it? Or maybe even that movie *Ghost Ship*, where everyone gets cut in half in the first scene?* Did an entire party die in that ballroom? Was the band gunned down in a hellish musical assassination? When that band strikes up, are there invisible dancers cutting a rug all around us?

But okay, moving past the band, consider that there are times, when all else is quiet, when from the part of the building that used to house a morgue you can hear a baby crying. We don't even need to talk about the possibilities there: there's a ghostly baby crying in an old morgue; leave it at that and let your imagination fill in the hideous gaps.

If you head upstairs at the Royal, you can make your way to Room 5, which is as haunted a room as ever a room was haunted. The hotel staff themselves try not to go into Room 5 if they can help it: if you can spend a night in it without losing your marbles, all power to you, for the room is filled with lost souls seeking a solid body to commune with, to terrify or simply to take out a century's worth of repressed anger on. Not that Room 5 is dangerous, unless you consider going insane to be a danger.

And yet not even Room 5, with its chill air, malevolent presence and floating faces, is the worst of the Royal Hotel. For Seymour's greatest, most unspeakable horror is to be found outside the hotel itself, in the stables. Not even the ghost tour will take customers out there, for in the stables there is something so horrific, and happenings so appalling,

---

* That was so cool.

that nobody can even speak of them. At least, they won't speak of them to me. I'm trying not to take it personally. Suffice it to say that if a trip to the Royal Hotel begins with some jolly poltergeisting in the bar, if you're not careful where you stray, it might end in hell.

Gone for Goodna

Ipswich, Queensland

It is said that Goodna Cemetery, in Ipswich, Queensland, is one of the most haunted cemeteries in Australia, which is saying something, because when it comes to haunting, cemeteries tend to be prime locations, and a hell of a lot of them have a little bit of paranormal activity buzzing about. Even the ones without actual ghosts can call themselves haunted in a figurative sense, so Goodna is really up against stiff competition. There's no doubt, though, that it's done itself proud.

One reason for this is that Goodna is the cemetery that at one point served the old Ipswich Mental Asylum – and, as we are well aware, asylums are great ghost factories due to the fact that historically they've tended to treat their patients abominably, and anyone who dies in one is likely to have been incredibly pissed off when they did so. This, apparently, is the case at Goodna, where about two hundred former residents of the asylum are buried, and where, should you make your unwary way among the gravestones, you may feel the hands of those aggrieved souls attempting to grapple with the material world.

People walking through the cemetery have reported being grabbed by invisible hands and scratched by invisible fingernails: graveyard denizens trying to expel the living from their turf – or maybe trying to drag them back to the grave with them? Whatever the motive, visitors have left Goodna Cemetery with cuts, scratches and bruises on their skin, the invisible assailants not holding back their savage attacks.

It is said that if you cover your car with flour and drive past the cemetery – okay, I know that would be a weird thing to do, but it's an experiment, hear me out – you will, upon alighting from the vehicle, discover that it is covered all over with fingerprints. The cemetery's people are reaching out to you ... and not in a good way. Think of what those fingers were trying to do ... and what could happen, if one were to forget to wind one's windows up before setting out.

There is one story told of Goodna Cemetery that is so fantastic it sounds exactly like the sort of tale you tell around a campfire to scare children. Luckily, it's completely true, so there's no need to see it that way.

The story concerns one man who drove to Goodna – without any flour on his car – to pay his respects to a departed friend. Once within the grounds of the graveyard, the man found himself subject to the famed abuses of the Goodna ghouls. Pushed and shoved, pummelled and scratched, he thought it was about time to get the hell out of there, and so scurried back to his car and started the engine.

But when he slammed his foot on the accelerator, the car didn't move. In a panic, the man pressed the gas over and over. The engine revved loudly. The wheels spun in place and churned up the turf. He checked and rechecked his gearstick. Everything seemed to be in order, the car was running perfectly, but no matter what the driver did – It. Would. Not. Move.

All night the man sat in his car, the doors locked, trying and failing to get it moving as the grim atmosphere of the cemetery seemed to close in evermore. After hours of near-heartbursting terror, the sun began to rise, and suddenly, as he once again turned the key and put his foot down, the car sprang forward. The poor fellow nearly had a stroke from sheer relief, but managed to speed away and get safely home.

After pulling into his driveway in the pale morning sunshine, the man got out of the car, turned and nearly fainted. For on the sides of the vehicle, running its whole length from fender to fender, was a series of huge gashes in the metal. Deep, angry furrows, as if massive claws had taken hold of the machine and been holding it in place. All night long.

The Kindly Matron

Beechworth, Victoria

The Beechworth Lunatic Asylum operated on the traditional system used by colonial asylums, known popularly as the 'Easy to Get In, Good Luck Getting Out' system. The possibility for abuse of this approach may have occurred to the administrators of the asylum, but they were much too busy taking advantage of the possibilities for abuse everywhere else in the place.

The institution opened in 1867 on a hill above the historic town of Beechworth. The location was selected in the hope that the brisk winds at altitude would help blow away the patients' afflictions, so you can guess just how rigorous the staff's commitment to sound scientific principles were. The asylum's first superintendent, Doctor Thomas Dick – a powerful example of nominative determinism – believed that the moon caused insanity, so would never go outside at night without an umbrella. Just to be clear: this was the man who was in charge of *treating* mental illness.

As for the treatment, it wasn't what you might call TLC. It wasn't until the 1950s that medication was first used, so for most of its existence patients spent a lot of time in straitjackets or even chains, and were more likely to be subjected to electro-shock therapy or surgery than a talking cure. The results of the surgeries are believed to still be in the asylum somewhere: jars of body parts in formaldehyde that were apparently walled up in the cellar as a disgusting surprise for future researchers.

Between the shackling and the electrocuting and the dismembering, it wasn't a happy place to be, but the ghosts who hang around there today don't seem to be holding any grudges. In the electro-shock wing, a little girl has been seen kneeling in the dark, most likely praying that there'd be a power cut. Elsewhere, a doctor, showing incredible commitment to duty decades after his death, roams the halls and checks up on long-gone patients.

Meanwhile, outside in the garden strolls Arthur in his green jacket. Arthur used to work in the asylum's garden, wearing the same jacket no matter the weather. After he died, £140 was found sewn into the jacket's seams: life savings from his ten shillings a week that never did poor Arthur any good.

The sweetest inhabitant of the old madhouse, though, is Matron Sharpe. From back in the days when the Beechworth Asylum was still a going concern, staff and patients would catch sight of this kindly lady, who had overseen the wards years before with far more kindness and compassion than anyone would've expected. Matron Sharpe could be seen walking the halls and stairways, but her presence was particularly noted when patients underwent the notorious shock therapy. The ghost of the matron would appear to sit with the patient and grant them comfort. When Sharpe was present, the room became freezing cold, but patients were reassured by her presence. It seems that, just as she had in life, Matron Sharpe knew the inmates of the asylum needed her; she wouldn't let death stop her from being there for them.

It can therefore be confidently stated that of all the ghost matrons of abandoned asylums in Australia, Matron Sharpe is the nicest. Compared to the strangling matron of Picton, for example, she comes out well ahead. In fact, if you're after a haunting experience with a touch of compassion, you could do worse than head to the Beechworth Lunatic Asylum, where a legacy of torture and horrific abuse has produced a rather sweet-natured phantom matron, an amiable old gent in a green jacket and a few other sundry ghosts who mostly mind their own business. As long as you can overlook the disembodied sounds of running, laughing children, you'll have a great time.

The Drunken Spectre of Breakfast Creek

Brisbane, Queensland

The first thing to get out of the way is that, no, the Breakfast Creek Hotel does not serve breakfast. This is extremely disappointing, but it's not the only thing about the place to defy rational explanation. The hotel was named after the Breakfast Creek, which was named after the time two guys had breakfast with some Aboriginal people, one of whom then tried to steal one of the two guys' hats.* This has nothing to do with ghosts, but it seems worth knowing.

The hotel rises magnificently over Kingsford Smith Drive in Brisbane, a building of spectacular and intricate ornamentation in the French Renaissance style. Cornices and parapets and verandahs and balustrades and fancy columns abound. It's an impressive pile, and this is precisely what you'd expect because it was originally built for William McNaughton Galloway, one-time mayor of Brisbane and amateur Ned Kelly impersonator. Galloway had two great dreams: to build a beautiful hotel and to grow a beard longer than a freshwater crocodile. He achieved both and is an inspiration to us all.

But there was a dark side to William Galloway, and that dark side is what caused him to end up a somewhat chastened ghost hanging around his old pub and making people uncomfortable.

The thing is, Galloway liked a drink. Now, that is not such a big deal:

---

* History comes alive!

most people like a drink. In Queensland, even more people like a drink than usual. And in 1890s Queensland, even more people liked a drink than they do now. Plus, Galloway owned a hotel, so it was unlikely that he would have a hostile relationship with liquor.

But old William, he REALLY liked a drink. To put it more accurately, he liked a great number of drinks, consumed in quick succession. On Saturday 12 January 1895, he had been knocking them back at a steady clip for three straight weeks, and his nearest and dearest were understandably concerned. Seeing the boss was drunk again, William Floyd, the Breakfast Creek bartender, had a brainwave: he'd lock Galloway in a room upstairs, safely away from the punters, and let him sleep it off.

It was an excellent plan except for one flaw: the room he used had a window, and Galloway was not the kind of pub proprietor / occasional mayor to just sit quietly and accept imprisonment. Exiting the window onto a ledge, he sought to complete his daring escape by springing nimbly onto the balcony that protruded from the wall a little way along. But he did not spring nimbly. In fact, he sprang in very much the way you might expect an intoxicated middle-aged man to spring. He did just well enough to catch hold of the balcony railing, but failed at his next task: hanging on. Hands slipping from the rail, he plummeted to the ground and died shortly afterwards.

Above the stairs at the Breakfast Creek Hotel is a stained-glass window depicting Lady Macbeth, so it should be clear to all that this is a hotel that from the start expected to be haunted. So the death of its founder, though of course a terrible tragedy, was in a sense the fulfilment of the pub's destiny. And it was on those very stairs, creepily overseen as they are by one of fiction's greatest accessories before the fact, that the return of the former proprietor was first noticed. A dark shadow was seen ascending the stairs, and on the landing an unearthly glow appeared. The Breakfast Creek Hotel was officially haunted, and it was about time.

Since then, old man Galloway has frequently made his presence felt, bringing with him a chill in the air and an indefinable sense of overdoing it. He spends a lot of time in his old room, looming out of the darkness to frighten people who pop in, and looking at the window muttering, 'I still think I could make it' over and over again. But he is also known to wander the public areas of the hotel and has become a familiar sight to Breakfast Creek staff, who gain a certain sense of security from knowing that, more than one hundred and twenty years after he took his fatal spill, the big, bearded bugger still cares enough to come in to work.

The Dame of Dunolly

Dunolly, Victoria

Dunolly was born from the gold rush, springing up in the 1850s in the middle of the Victorian goldfields. By 1861, the Criterion Hotel had been built to lubricate the dry throats of the miners and cash in on the rush itself. Today, the Criterion has been renamed the Railway Hotel, but it retains its quaint Victorian charm, along with its quaint Victorian ghosts.

Beneath the Railway Hotel lies, as seems logical, its cellar, a wide space lined with ancient stones, where the cool, musty air can make a person feel taken out of time, dislocated to the gold rush, when the greedy and the desperate scrabbled in the dirt for their one big chance, while rough and violent men lay in wait nearby to scoop up the spoils for themselves. And although, when you put it like that, it sounds terribly romantic, you've got to remember that a lot of people had really horrible diseases as well.

Down in the cellar, along with old wooden shelves and empty dust-covered bottles, is a sealed-up doorway that once led into a rabbit's warren of tunnels that snake through the goldfields' soil. What blackguards stooped to make their way through those tunnels, skinning elbows on the walls and jumping at the shadows cast by lonely candles? What dark crimes were hidden there, what secrets buried, what dreadful stories reached their conclusion deep beneath the pub's

211

floorboards, far from the sun? Only the ghosts who drift through the dust could tell you, and they are silent.

If one spirit might know some of the Railway Hotel's secrets, perhaps it is the old lady upstairs: a veteran of the hotel's earliest days who wanders the halls in a state of mild irritation at all the intruders, and at the fact that she's no longer in charge. In the olden days she dealt with drunken diggers, bar-room brawls and all the clashes and carouses to which a frontier pub is accustomed. Now she is powerless, quite literally a shadow of her former self, and must deal with both the impotence of insubstantiality and the frustration of being tethered to her old workplace.

Everyone in Dunolly knows the stories of the Railway's old lady, and it's mostly newcomers to town whom she disturbs. She likes to sit upstairs and gaze out the window at the bustling activity of the town, living vicariously through, well, the living. You might not even notice she's there unless you get in her way. But then she will make her presence felt in no uncertain terms.

Countless guests of the old hotel have gone up to their room and, ready for a well-earned rest after driving all the way from the city with broken air-conditioning, sat down on the bed. Which, as it turns out, in the Railway Hotel is a big mistake, because no sooner have their buttocks sunk gratefully onto the doona than they are suddenly shoved off violently.

It's the old lady, furious that yet another interloper has blocked her view. The bed, you see, is where *she* sits, to look out the window and dream of the days when she had a body. It can be even more startling if someone chooses to lie down, as she'll roll them right onto the floor, with the strength of a ghost who used to spend many hours manhandling miners.

This makes the Railway Hotel a unique offering in the hospitality world. For people looking for a peaceful night's rest, it's a risky proposition, but for anyone wanting a personal connection to the heady days of the gold rush, it can't be beaten.

The Kangaroo Horses

Maldon, Victoria

The Kangaroo Hotel's website makes the boast that it is 'the only Kangaroo Hotel in Australia', which is something to hang your hat on, I suppose. Possibly all the other hotels decided not to name themselves the Kangaroo Hotel in case people thought it was a hotel *for* kangaroos, and therefore decided not to give it their human custom. So, for the sake of their business, let me assure you that the uniquely monikered Kangaroo Hotel, in the High Street of Maldon, right across the road from Elsie and Pat's Antiques and just down the road from the Bill Woodfull Recreation Reserve, definitely does serve humans. And in all likelihood it wouldn't serve kangaroos even if they did show up there.

The Kangaroo Hotel was built in 1856, the same year the little goldfields settlement officially became the town of Maldon. The hotel started life as a tent, but quickly grew in grandeur, just like the town itself. Early on, Maldon was a boom town, servicing thousands of miners at the nearby Tarrangower Fields. When the reefs were mined out, the town dwindled somewhat, but today it's a popular artists' retreat and tourist destination, of interest for its historic architecture and ghost horses. So … okay, bear with me.

Maldon, besides serving as a goldfields hub, was also an important stop along the road from Bendigo, to the north-east, to Ballarat and Melbourne. The Kangaroo Hotel itself was for some time a Cobb & Co.

changing station, its stables seeing a steady rotation of fine horseflesh. Sadly, it was those stables that were at the centre of the pub's greatest tragedy, and its persistent haunting.

It was the 1870s, after the boom times had faded, and Maldon had settled down into being a cosy country town rather than a thriving metropolis on rivers of gold. The coaches continued to rattle through town on the regular, though, and the horses were always treated well at the Kangaroo Hotel. Until one terrible, terrible night.

Nobody knew how it started. Perhaps a lantern was knocked onto some straw. Perhaps a careless stablehand dropped his cigarette. Maybe there was foul play by some twisted miscreant. Whatever the origin, the fact is that while the Kangaroo Hotel rang with the sounds of revelry and well-quenched thirsts, the nearby stables had caught alight and the horses were rearing wildly in their stalls.

At some point the crackling flames and billowing smoke were noticed, and the alarm sounded. The hotel staff and townsfolk rushed to fight the blaze, frantically filling buckets of water as great red and orange tongues licked greedily at the night sky. From within the stables could be heard a horrific cacophony of horses screaming and pounding walls and doors with their hooves.

Crazed with panic as the stables crumbled and fell around them, some of the animals managed to find their way through the blinding smoke and hellish heat to bolt into the cool of the night. But others never made it out alive. With rescue efforts coming too late, they succumbed, either overcome by the heat or choked by the smoke. When at last the fire was out and the people picked their way through the black, smoking ruins of the stables, they found ten lifeless bodies lying where they'd fallen in overwhelming fear and pain. A more horrible sight they couldn't recall seeing.

These days, when visitors to Maldon come in by car or on the Goldfields Railway from Castlemaine, no one needs to change their horses at the Kangaroo Hotel. But the reminder of the days of Cobb & Co. is there, in the ghosts that haunt the old pub. Not human ghosts, but the unhappy spirits of those ten poor beasts which perished that night.

Come to the ol' Kangaroo and you will hear them, whinnying, snorting, stamping their feet in the yard. You may hear their clopping hooves outside the window, or – if you take a walk around the yard where the stables once stood – even feel their warm breath on your face, or a heavy body brush past you in the dark. Stay late into the night and you may even find your spine tingling as the faint smell of smoke drifts to your nostrils, the distant sound of crackling flames reaches your ear and, somewhere within, the terrified screams of trapped animals echo.

Raise a glass to those noble beasts, who lived and died in the service of the people of the old goldfields.

O Fortuna

Bendigo, Victoria

George Lansell was what we call 'a big deal'. A very big deal. In fact, the thriving city of Bendigo would not be what it is today had it not been for George Lansell – and though you might say that's a good reason to curse his name, that's a terribly uncharitable point of view and you should be ashamed of yourself. For Lansell did a lot for Bendigo, and if it so happens that he did that lot while in the process of also doing a lot for himself, well, a man's gotta make a living. His position in the town can be seen in the statue of him that still stands today.

Lansell came to Bendigo in 1854 to open a shop selling soap and candles, but fairly soon realised that an even better idea would be to become a fabulously wealthy mining tycoon, so he did that instead. He began by investing in unsuccessful quartz-mining companies and losing his money, but when he had the brainwave of investing in successful quartz-mining companies and making money, his fortunes turned around rapidly.

George Lansell became known as the 'Quartz King of Bendigo', even though he had no hereditary claim to the title. He purchased, expanded and renovated the house named Fortuna Villa, turning the splendid mansion into an even more splendid mansion, furnished with the finest pieces from around the globe and set amid lavish lawns and lakes.

The magnificence of Fortuna Villa is still apparent to this day to anyone who visits, but over the years it has become clear that there is more than just architecture to dazzle and amaze there. So prevalent are paranormal palavers at the house that from 1942, when the Department of Defence took possession of the property, the staff started the 'Fortuna Ghost Book', with any unexplained occurrences noted down in it.

Among these were the time an officer spotted a glowing, spinning orb floating in the grounds, popping in and out of sight before drifting through the kitchen wall and vanishing for good. It was later found that the spot on which the orb was initially seen was the location of a soldier's suicide.

Elsewhere in the villa can be found the Perfume Ghost, a lady who used to be governess to the Lansell children. Her presence can be detected through the sudden inexplicable scent of perfume wafting through a room. Less fragrant and more unsettling is the head and torso of a man that has been seen passing through solid objects in the house, or the young soldier who once appeared hanging from a rope at the end of another soldier's bed.

Most skin-crawling of all, however, is the young woman who, throughout the defence force's stay at Fortuna, pleaded constantly for them to leave. The woman was invisible, but it became a common experience for staff at the villa to feel her creep up behind them and whisper in their ear, 'Who are you? What do you want? Please leave.'

It's testament to the bravery of our men and women in uniform that they didn't clear out then and there, but one can't help feeling sorry for the poor young woman who so dearly wished to be left alone. Alas, such is often the lot of ghosts – the location and circumstances of your haunting are rarely in your control, and the living rarely get out of your way.*

If there is much to disturb and unsettle among the phantoms of Fortuna, there is at least one more solid and calming spectre hanging about. George Lansell passed away in 1906 and was much mourned,

---

* Actually, the living not getting out of your way is a big problem for the living as well.

with flags across Bendigo flying at half-mast. From the day he died, there were sightings of him drifting about Fortuna, in particular haunting the lookout tower, where he can be seen, aptly enough, looking out over the goldfields that once were his. In a white jacket and straw boater, and wielding his old walking stick, he still cuts a dapper figure, and lets all who come to Fortuna know that the Quartz King still dwells in his castle.

The Angry Matron

York, Western Australia

The corridor of the Old York Hospital stretched away, dark and empty and forbidding. White walls with grim doors set in them, looking more like a prison than a hospital. Today the wards were silent – it had been years since anyone had been brought there to get well. And looking at the place, it was hard to believe anyone ever came out of it feeling better than when they went in.

Two boys had snuck into the abandoned building to see what the big deal was. The younger lad knew as soon as he entered that he was being watched. His hair stood on end as he felt hundreds of eyes upon him, tracking his every move. He begged his older companion to leave, but the bigger boy insisted on exploring further. He started up the stairs.

There was a great scream as the older boy threw himself back down the stairs, landing right on his friend. 'Let's go, let's go,' he shrieked. Both of them bolted. Outside, the older told the younger that on the stairs he had felt a hand stroke his head.

Old York Hospital was built in 1896, to care for sick miners in the West Australian goldfields. In 1963 the hospital closed, later becoming a youth hostel for many years.

At the top of the building is a room that, when the hospital was operational, no one dared go into alone. The nurses knew that upstairs was something awful, waiting to pounce. As far back as the 1920s, the hospital was home to a dark and angry presence.

Later on, guests staying at the hostel were tormented by that same *something*. In the kitchen, teapots and plates would rise into the air, float across the room and crash to the ground. In the night, someone would moan long and loud, causing icicles to form in the veins of listeners. On the stairs, blood flowed from nowhere, trickling down and pooling on the ground floor. Ghastly figures drifted down hallways and through walls, noiseless but with expressions of agony and fear etched on their faces.

Anyone who stayed there developed a powerful desire to vacate the premises as soon as possible. On one particularly grim occasion, the resident spirit lost patience with a party on its turf. Venting its fury, it lifted an eight-year-old girl bodily off the ground and threw her through a glass door. She need fifteen stitches and a lifetime of therapy.

What was in the Old York Hospital that brought such terror and distress to anyone who entered? Whence came the dark, malicious energy that turned a house of healing into a house of horrors? Who was in the hospital, and why were they so angry?

In the institution's early days, so the story goes, the matron of the hospital was the victim of a horrific crime. Raped in that room upstairs, she stayed behind after her death, forever seeking the man who had attacked her in order to wreak her revenge. In the meantime, filled with rage and hatred, she takes it out on anyone who crosses her path.

After years of hearing stories of the angry matron and the disturbing happenings at the old hospital, the National Trust disowned the site in 1998. Nobody wants to go near the place, and those who do are cured of their curiosity remarkably quickly. One must presume that the matron still walks the corridors, burning with vengeful fire and looking for the perpetrator of the outrage. But it is a search that will never reach its culmination, and the spirit will therefore remain forever in those long, dark, threatening halls.

The Haunted Castle

Black Rock, Victoria

There is a secret tunnel underneath Black Rock House that winds its way to the beach. Perhaps it is a smugglers' tunnel, built to dodge customs. Perhaps it is an escape tunnel, dug out to give the inhabitants of the old house a way to evade those who'd do them harm. Some still remember crawling up it, the awful smell and the dank, dark, claustrophobic silence pressing in on you. Some say that people have drowned in there when the tide was high.

Black Rock House, sitting by Port Phillip Bay in Melbourne's suburbs, was built by Charles Ebden, the filthy rich pastoralist and first auditor-general of Victoria, who made the place his holiday home. He modelled it on Blackrock Castle in Ireland, hence the unnecessary ramparts and medieval accoutrements. It was known locally as Castle Ebden, and its looming Gothic facade proved useful for setting imaginations running wild as to what terrors dwelled within. Particularly when you factored in things like secret tunnels and smugglers – and, why the hell not, pirates maybe?

There are said to be thirteen ghosts in Black Rock House, making the air thick with other-worldly dread and eldritch frissons. The most outgoing is the young woman who welcomes male company and who will attach herself to young men who come visiting, hoping for some companionship and affection.

Other residents are not as gregarious. A popular destination for those who come to Black Rock specifically seeking the uncanny is the 'death room'. This room got its name partly for marketing purposes, but partly also because people who enter it are overwhelmed by the sensation of death. A putrid stench reaches their nostrils, as if some animal had perished here. Those who sit on the bed are stung by a pain in the head and the sudden conviction that someone died in that very spot. Some feel seasick and lose their balance; others find themselves unable to enter the room at all, blocked by some invisible barrier. Who died in the death room, and who lurks there still to plague visitors, is unknown.

In the hallway of Black Rock House, dark shadows have been seen darting from room to room. Footsteps pace up and down the floor, the hall alive with the echoes of people who once bustled about the house. You may hear them coming towards you or walking quietly behind you. On occasion a voice has been heard, calling 'hello' to who knows who. Figures appear and disappear. Stand in a certain spot in the hallway and feel a chill come over you. Move to another and experience the crackle of unearthly electricity in the air. Stay stock-still and sense the house, as it seems, gently rocking from side to side. Or maybe it's just your imagination …

Maybe it's your imagination that someone just trudged, head bowed, past the other end of the hall. Maybe it's your imagination that, somewhere below you, there is a knocking and a scrabbling, as if someone were trying to escape. Maybe it's your imagination that invisible fingers are stroking your arm or ghostly breath is teasing the hairs on the back of your neck. Maybe it's your imagination that down in the cellar there is someone moving about, making bottles clink together.

It could all be your imagination, but few have set foot inside Black Rock House without finding their mind racing with the idea of thirteen ghosts circling them, swarming them, drawing them deeper towards the castle's eerie heart.

The Lady of the Theatre

Brisbane, Queensland

The Schonell Theatre was built in 1970, which some might think makes it an unlikely candidate for a haunting, given that ghosts tend to prefer more old-timey locales. Though it is possible that this author is now so old that he hasn't realised that 1970 is, in fact, the olden days, and his Led Zeppelin box set is nowhere near as cutting-edge as he thinks …

In any case, the Schonell Theatre *was* built in 1970, to celebrate the dissolution of the Beatles, and one can only assume that the location on which it was constructed had previously been occupied by some kind of terribly spooky old cottage or something. It is part of the University of Queensland, which is much older, so it's possible, but sad to say there is no way of knowing exactly where Sophea came from: only that she currently occupies the Schonell Theatre and that she is, by all accounts, quite a fun-loving gal.

Sophea is an attractive young woman wearing a full-length old-fashioned dress, such as might be seen on the television program *Downton Abbey*, so she falls into that category known by parapsychologists as 'ghosts that just look like people'. That is, when she appears, Sophea is not transparent or glowing or all green or anything: she just looks like an ordinary woman, which can make it quite difficult to spot her in a crowd. Especially if it's a crowd at a *Downton Abbey*–themed fancy dress party.

The question this raises is: is Sophea even an actual ghost, or is she just a weird lady who hangs around the theatre? This can be answered by a story told by a former theatre manager, who was standing with a colleague in the lobby after a show when a woman walked past them and into a dressing room. After waiting some time for her to re-emerge, they noticed that she didn't. Looking inside, they found the room empty, but it had no exits apart from the door she'd entered through – which would seem to be extremely suggestive, would it not? Yes, it would. That was Sophea, retiring for the evening.

In general, Sophea does not appear before members of the public, but has become well loved by the Schonell Theatre staff. Managers, cleaners, maintenance workers and other employees have seen her often, and even more often have encountered her in non-visual ways: for Sophea does not always go around dressed in her body; most of the time she stays invisible, presumably to save battery power. But the sound of her footsteps echoing around the theatre after a show has become familiar to all.

Sophea doesn't seem to be the angsty kind of ghost, as she shows no interest in jumping out or screaming at people, or in wailing over the terrible tragedy that reduced her to this state. Instead, she likes to play games. One cleaner would often find that after she had thrown away a piece of paper, it would pop up again in the same spot. She would clean it away again, and again it would return. Only after the cleaner firmly told Sophea, 'Stop it!' did the game come to an end, which shows that Sophea is not only a playful lass, but also respectful of others' boundaries. And let's face it, you can't say that of many ghosts.

Of course, it's well known that all the best theatres have resident ghosts, and Schonell is proud that, for a modest little venue, it's got such a charismatic and friendly haunter. For anyone who would like to be in the presence of a ghost but would prefer not to be scared witless by creepy dead children or awakened by cold invisible hands tightening around their throat, Schonell Theatre is definitely the place to go. But make sure you hang around after the show is finished: remember, Sophea gets a bit shy.

Nellie's Final Encore

Melbourne, Victoria

The stately Hotel Windsor rises in Victorian splendour, overlooking Spring Street in the heart of Melbourne. Though other buildings in the CBD might match its grandeur, none surpasses it, and within its venerable walls is contained a temple of high luxury. With a proud history dating back to 1884, and an opulence seldom found elsewhere, the Windsor's guest list over the years has, unsurprisingly, boasted many names of high renown. Margaret Thatcher, Don Bradman, Meryl Streep, Muhammad Ali, George VI and an array of Australian prime ministers are just a few of the notables who have enjoyed the prompt room service and fluffy towels of the Windsor.

But perhaps no guest of the Windsor has greater significance than Dame Nellie Melba, the world-famous opera singer and toast-inspirer who put Australia on the map as a nation of high culture rather than simply a giant desert island full of flies and murderers. At least, no guest of the Windsor has greater significance to a compiler of ghost stories. Because good luck trying to make contact with the spirit of Maggie Thatcher in the tea rooms: if you want a truly classy and genteel paranormal experience at the Hotel Windsor, it's Dame Nellie you're going to want to see.

Nellie Melba's real name was Helen Porter Mitchell, but she gave herself the surname 'Melba' after her home town of Melbourne, which she apparently thought was called 'Melba'. Despite this, she did forever carry a fondness for the city, and, later in life, having conquered Europe and America with her fancy warbling, she frequently returned. When she was in the city, the Windsor was her preferred place to stay, and it was also where she returned after her death.[*]

There is a young boy who has often been seen loitering around level one of the Windsor: a teenage ghost who, it is believed, is guarding Melba's room. Dame Nellie was a woman of fierce and unquenchable passions, and she was known to indulge in those passions in the Windsor. Often, she would meet lovers in the hotel, paying staff for their silence.[†] This boy would seem to be the ghost of a lad she engaged to keep watch outside her room and make sure she wasn't disturbed during her assignations.

What this suggests, of course, is that even in her afterlife, Nellie Melba is getting some. But how do we even know that she's there? The answer is simply that we can hear her sing. Late at night, guests and staff alike have heard soaring arias being belted out joyously, filling the hotel with heavenly music. Windsor insiders are in no doubt that the voice is Dame Nellie's: how many other ghosts could let rip in such a flawless soprano? Given the presence of the boy outside her room, it has also been suggested that her singing might be her way of indicating her satisfaction with whatever gentleman ghost she is currently entertaining. Either that or the ghostly singing is the ethereal echo of the real thing, recorded by the atmospheric ectoplasm in the hotel … or something.

The Windsor is a five-star hotel, and it's good to know that it can promise five-star ghosts as well. The presence of a national treasure like Nellie Melba in the place is proof not only of its excellent taste, but of its patriotism. No imported opera ghosts for the Windsor (unlike, just quietly, the Princess Theatre down the street): at this hotel, the spooks are homegrown, and that's something to be proud of.

---

[*] In a spiritual sense, I mean: she wasn't buried there or anything.

[†] Pretty dodgy that the staff needed to be paid for their silence. I mean, why couldn't they just be cool, you know?

Up on Spook Hill

Toowong, Queensland

On Avenue 12 of Toowong Cemetery, strange things have been going on. When the down-and-outs in the Great Depression slept in the graveyard, and the lights flashed above their heads and the noises from nowhere woke them, it was around Avenue 12 that it happened. When ghost soldiers overran the cemetery, they appeared on Avenue 12. When a bell chimed at midnight from the grave of the great boxer Peter Jackson, and the great fighter rose from his grave with gloves up, ready for one more round, it was right by Avenue 12. When the vanishing fox stared into your eyes and tried to get you to follow it, it was on Avenue 12. And when the beautiful woman with the long, shining fangs walked between the tombstones, it was along Avenue 12 that she strolled.

For Avenue 12 is the road that runs down Spook Hill, and from Spook Hill the horrors come out to play.

Once, years and years ago, two young sisters went out on the town in Brisbane and never came home. Their car crashed and both girls were killed, and the public grief was terrible. They were buried at Toowong, the last resting place of Prime Minister Frank Forde, Brisbane's first mayor, John Petrie, and Walter Porriott, who may or may not have been Jack the Ripper. And, of course, the great Jackson. It was a prestigious place for the sisters to be interred, and they were given prime position, right on top of a hill – the popular name of which was not, presumably, known to the girls' parents at the time.

Struck down by a reckless driver in the prime of life, the sisters were not pleased to be killed, and since they were buried they haven't got any happier. They are sad about the life that was denied to them. They are angry at the world that snuffed them out so young. And perhaps more than anything … they are lonely. For there is no company in a grave, and even when you're buried alongside your sibling, conversation can drag after a few decades.

This is why, if you happen one night to take a wrong turn into Toowong Cemetery – and honestly, try not to – don't drive down Avenue 12. Because those sisters are waiting. And from up on Spook Hill, they're drawing you in …

Cars have stopped at the bottom of Spook Hill, and their drivers have felt terror suffocate them as the car – slowly at first, but accelerating relentlessly – begins to *roll up the hill*. And once your vehicle begins rolling up the hill, you are in a world of trouble. Hit the brakes all you want. Change gear to your heart's content. You've as much chance to escape as the Millennium Falcon in the Death Star's tractor beam, and there's something even nastier waiting at the end of the trip.

The best thing you can do is to open the door, dive out and roll. Or, if you find that the doors are mysteriously locked and resistant to your attempts to open them, try to break a window. And once you're out, run as hard and as fast as you can, down that hill and as far away as possible, before the invisible winch that's reeling in your car gets hold of you too.

Because it's those angry, lonely sisters who are dragging you up the hill, and they are determined to pull you down into the grave with them. Whatever dark energy possesses that hill, the girls have harnessed it in their long and desperate search for new souls to keep them company. If they had their way, every passer-by foolish enough to wander down Avenue 12 would end their journey alongside them, deep, deep down in the cold ground … up on Spook Hill.

The Tragedy of Point Cook

Point Cook, Victoria

About twenty kilometres south-west of Melbourne can be found Point Cook, and the homestead that bears its name. The graceful bluestone house was built by the Chirnside brothers, Thomas and Andrew, who came to Australia from Scotland and made fortunes in sheep, back in the days when Australia rode on that particular mammal's back. Later, they would build a grander mansion at Werribee Park, which became a home for Andrew's family. Thomas stayed at Point Cook, and is seemingly still there now.

The Point Cook Homestead seems to have been cursed from the beginning. Glimpses of wandering ghosts have long been reported, departed souls come to violent ends now bound to the place. On the nearby beach there once washed up the drowned body of a sixteen-year-old boy, his wrists bound. Police decided there was no foul play, because this was back in the days when they had an impish sense of humour.

Certainly, one of the spirits floating about Point Cook must be Tommy the groom, who died in the stables. The Chirnside brothers were famed breeders of high-class thoroughbreds, including one Melbourne Cup winner, and the stables at Point Cook were usually full of expensive horseflesh. It was just before the 1876 Cup that the prize horse Newminster was poisoned, and suspicion fell on young Tommy. The lad had been seen, allegedly, shaking hands with a bookmaker days earlier, and quite logically he was blamed for the outrage. Whether the accusations were true or not would never be tested: Tommy was found hanging in the stables not long afterwards.

Perhaps he took his own life out of guilt, or from despair at being falsely accused. Or perhaps he was murdered to ensure his silence. We can't know. But you may still see him at a window, or walking through the yard at Point Cook.

The most prominent of the homestead's resident phantoms is Thomas Chirnside himself. He will be seen, dressed to the nines, wandering the house or strolling in the gardens, overseeing the property he built and was for so long master of. He walks alone, for in death it seems that Thomas is as lonely as he was in life, and the sight of him walking endlessly is as sad as the story that brought him there.

After establishing himself in Australia, Thomas returned for a time to Scotland, where he fell in love with his cousin Mary – but it was alright because it was the olden days and people really didn't mind that sort of thing. He asked Mary to come back to Australia with him, but she refused and he sailed back alone.

Later, his brother Andrew also journeyed to Scotland. 'Please, brother,' asked Thomas, 'while you are there, beg my Mary to reconsider, and to come back with you to marry me.' Andrew agreed, and when he returned to Australia, Mary was indeed with him – but she had married Andrew.

It was with a stoicism both admirable and heartbreaking that the devastated Thomas watched his brother make a home at Werribee Park Mansion, start a family and raise six children with the woman he loved. But he carried on, uncomplaining. He continued building his business, he gave to charity and built a church in Werribee.

But he never married. While Andrew and his family prospered at the mansion, Thomas stayed at Point Cook Homestead, all alone. In his old age he became sick and depressed. Although still a wealthy man, he began to believe himself plagued by huge debts. He gave most of his estate to his brother and nephews, but grew convinced that he was bankrupt. Despairing, in 1887, at the age of seventy-two, Thomas Chirnside shot himself while visiting the house at Werribee Park.

It's no wonder that his ghost, melancholy and bereft, still graces his beloved homestead. And no wonder that women, visiting the place, have reported feeling somehow unwelcome when entering his old bedroom. For, after all, there only ever was one woman that Thomas Chirnside wished to shared that room with.

The Gallows Ghosts

Brisbane, Queensland

The oldest building in Brisbane is the Old Windmill on Wickham Terrace. Built in 1828 to grind grain, it was useful as a source of both food and torment for the local convicts: when there was no wind to drive the sails, the mill was powered by a treadmill on which convicts would trudge to make their own flour. After its life as a windmill expired, the tower served as a signal station, a fire tower, a museum, a broadcasting tower and a weather observatory. But for our purposes, its most significant period was the day it served as a gallows.

The most morbid part of the Old Windmill's history stemmed, originally, from the settlement of the Moreton Bay region itself, when a bunch of enthusiastic white chaps showed up and decided this would be a splendid place to live, and a bunch of equally enthusiastic black chaps raised the issue that they were already living there. In fact, they considered the place rather precious. Obviously, the white chaps were sympathetic to this point of view, but they had to weigh the deep connection that the original inhabitants had to the land against the fact that they really, really wanted the land for themselves.

The upshot was that the Europeans took the land and forced the Aboriginal population off it, and that the Aboriginal population, with a certain amount of the moral high ground under their feet, fought back. In one of the frequent clashes between white settlers and the Indigenous resistance, the reasonably nasty surveyor Granville Stapylton and a convict in his survey party named William Tuck were speared to death, burned and mutilated, and their camp looted.

The colonial authorities went in search of the culprits, and two Aboriginal men, named Mullan and Ningavil, were put on trial for murder. James Dunlop, who had been with the survey party and survived the attack, testified that the two men weren't the killers, but they had been wearing clothes stolen from the camp and so were condemned to death.

The Old Windmill was thus pressed into service as an instrument of execution. On 3 July 1841, a beam was put out of an upper window and a rope hung from it down to the balcony, from which the prisoners were pushed. It was a short drop, and the men were slowly strangled as they swung on the ends of the ropes: a peculiarly horrible mode of death. The ten-year-old son of Brisbane's foreman of works was taken to the coffin of one of the executed and looked at his face. His daughter would later write, 'The horror of the ghastly sight so frightened the child that it set him crying, and he could not get over it.'

The convict era passed away, but the Old Windmill still stood, as it does to this day. A city sprang up around the structure, and as more and more people took up residence near the tower, more and more people began reporting that something there was … off.

For sometimes, when one observed the little window that overlooks Wickham Terrace, one could see an eerie glow.* And if one peered a little closer at the glow, one could see a figure in the window, swinging slowly from side to side … as if dangling from a rope.

Or, hey, maybe they're just dancing. That would be nice. But given the history of the Old Windmill – and indeed, you know, of the entire country – if you see a ghostly figure swinging from side to side, let's face it, your best bet is not a festive one.

---

* Probably most glows that you see from the windows of century-old buildings that are supposed to be uninhabited can be said to be 'eerie', so whether this glow was eerie in and of itself or whether it was just eerie due to its location is difficult to tell. To put it another way, would the glow have been eerie if it weren't in the window and just, say, in a cafe? These are questions history cannot answer.

The Ghost on Pinjarra Bridge

Pinjarra, Western Australia

With thanks to the journal of Mr Thomas Scott

It was the first of July, a year to the day since old Kate had died. One year since they had found her lying on the old bridge at Pinjarra, south of Perth. Dead, they said, of an apoplectic fit, but because they buried her the very next day, there was never any chance to find out for sure what had killed the old girl. But dead she was, and had been for twelve months, when the family were sat at home and Uncle John came in with a face as white as the moon outside, and proceeded tell a strange and terrible story.

'I have seen her!' he said, though when he told them who he had seen, and where, the rest struggled to believe that he had not been drinking. It was just then that there was heard at the back door three loud, heavy knocks. Unnerved by the coincidence, there was a commotion as everyone leaped to their feet and rushed to the door to see who was knocking. But when the door was opened, nobody could be seen: neither at the door nor as far as the eye could see on a still, cloudless night when the moon and stars shone bright in the sky.

Closing the door, they retreated into the house, trying to make sense of events. When all had settled back into their seats, there it came again: three knocks, booming and echoing off the walls. But this time, more: after the knocks came a voice, calling clearly, 'John!' And again: 'John!' And a third time.

234

With wild eyes they stared, a shiver running down every backbone, each face as white as Uncle John's had been when he first walked in. For they knew whose voice it was they had heard calling: it was Kate, and no mistake. Kate, who had been dead this past year: her voice they had heard, clear as a bell, outside the back door.

Uncle John raced again to the door, his eldest nephew following close behind. He threw the door open and looked desperately out. This time, there was no question who had been knocking, for before them, as large as life, was a woman – or at least the figure of one, glowing in the moonlight and drifting slowly away from the house. A tall, straight-backed woman she was, and wearing a light, loose dress of the type that old Kate had been wearing when she was found that fateful night a year before.

John stared at the vision, mouth opening and closing as if he were attempting to recall the power of speech, Finally the words came, in a low, shaking rasp. 'Yes,' he said. 'That is my sister Kate, or her apparition – which I saw on the old bridge.'

It was in the direction of the old bridge, a quarter mile from the farmhouse, that the vision was gliding. John reached out a hand and cried aloud, 'Kate!' As if the sound of her name had startled the spirit, it vanished instantly, leaving no trace. The two men were left standing, goggling, gibbering, in the empty yard.

The family gathered up their courage and went together, immediately, out to the old bridge. Bracing themselves for the terror of seeing Kate floating in the air before them, they were disappointed: there was no apparition. Back at the house, all stayed awake through the night, but saw and heard nothing more.

Yet three nights later, the vision of Kate once again was seen, floating serenely across the Pinjarra Bridge. Again the spirit was pursued; again it disappeared before anyone could get near it. It revealed itself several more times on successive nights, before the appearances ceased.

Until the next year. And the next. Indeed, from that first sighting onwards, every year the spectre would visit. For nine days just before and just after the anniversary of her death, old Kate would appear again on the old bridge, taking a stately walk across the Murray. Never did she stop or let anyone approach closely, yet year after year they saw her. It seems that for as many years hence as there are witnesses to watch, the ghost on Pinjarra Bridge will have her annual outing.

Pubkeeper of Mackay

Mackay, Queensland

It's called Langfords Hotel now, though it was previously known as the Railway Hotel. It stands on Tennyson Street, Mackay, and has done since 1908, surviving calamities such as the cyclone of 1918 and the chicken parma shortage of 1967.[*] It could be that the longevity of the old pub has something to do with the guardian spirit who watches over it.

Mackay's Railway Hotel was the first in Australia to have a female publican, back in the days when women weren't even allowed to vote. In fact, it was back in the days when women weren't technically even allowed in pubs, but one woman gave a stiff finger to that and ran the whole joint herself. Her name was Annie Lane and she was forced into the publican position by circumstance, when her husband ran afoul of the law and was taken out of circulation for a while. With the hotel already under construction, Annie had no choice but to step into the breach herself, and strike a blow for feminism while she was at it.

With such a history, it only seems fair that the spirit who watches over Langfords to this day is also a woman. Maybe it's the ghost of Annie Lane herself: you could understand her wanting to keep an eye on the place. Whoever she is, she's thorough.

Pete McGahan stayed at the hotel many years ago. As soon as he

---

[*]   I made one of those up. Guess which.

came up to his room to go to bed, he said, he got the feeling he wasn't alone. He put this down to the generous number of drinks he'd lately consumed, and not without reason: after all, as the saying goes, you're never alone with alcohol. As it turned out, he had company quite apart from the warm embrace of precious booze.

As Pete slipped into slumber, he was abruptly woken by a weight on his chest. Unable to sit up due to the pressure, he looked up to see a woman sitting on his bed, hands on his chest, pressing down.

Pete shook his head, trying to clear the grog fog he felt sure was responsible for the hallucination. But the woman remained. She wore a light blue dress and, according to Pete, 'I didn't feel as if she wanted to hurt me … I had the feeling she wanted help, like she wanted to ask me something.' Eventually the woman vanished, and Pete saw no sign of her, even after searching up and down the hotel corridor.

The next night, Pete made the supreme sacrifice and stayed sober before going to bed. It made no difference: the exact same thing happened. The lady in blue appeared and again seemed to need help. 'I can remember feeling as if she was asking me for something and it was urgent.' After another night in the hotel, Pete moved into his own house and never saw the lady in blue again.

Pete was just the latest in a long line of patrons to encounter this amiable lady, who walks through the rooms of the hotel each night, keeping a vigil over the pub and its guests. It's only after lights out that she appears, her pale blue dress shining in the darkness, the sound of her soft footsteps and gentle whispers echoing in the quiet night. She stops at the top of the stairs to look down, then continues her rounds along the corridor, checking that all is well.

At the end of her watch, she returns to the same room – second from the left, facing west. The room Pete McGahan was staying in. What kind of help she wants no one has yet worked out – but whatever it is, it must be for the good of the old Railway Hotel.

Crime and Punishment
in Geelong

Geelong, Victoria

The old Geelong Gaol is big and dark, and it looms over the landscape like a disapproving headmaster with cane in hand. It was built between 1849 and 1865, and operated until 1991, housing such distinguished guests in its time as Chopper Read, Squizzy Taylor and other dangerous men with made-up names. It was a popular place to send the very worst of the correctional community's denizens – the most violent of brutes, the most irredeemable of monsters – because Geelong Gaol was not an institution interested in rehabilitation. It was built for punishment, and punishment was what it distributed.

Only four men were hanged there, a surprisingly low number. But they didn't need a lot of hangings, because through disease, violence and murder, the prison more than made up its corpse quota. One in twenty inmates who entered its forbidding steel gates would come out feet first. Many of them left something behind: something that visitors to the now-decommissioned gaol have seen or heard or felt. And it's not just the inmates: there are those who are sure that old guards still stomp with ghostly boots along the corridors and walkways. It's only natural that they should, to make sure the ghosts of the prisoners stay in line. One guard in particular has been seen lurking by the central staircase and around the gallows: a slave to duty.

Voices, of course, echo throughout the old gaol: what kind of an abandoned prison would it be if they didn't? Moans and curses fill the air at night; footsteps clatter and thud. But you're lucky if scary noises are all you're subjected to: the figures of long-deceased criminals have been seen hanging about in the shadows, and will on occasion actually attack the living who cross their paths. Visitors have been grabbed, scratched, pushed and had their hair pulled in the gaol.

The worst spot for aggressive spirits is Cell 45, but only if you're a woman: whoever is still 'living' there shows no interest in men – and whatever disturbing conclusions you want to make about the ghost's activities in life, go ahead. If a woman is unwary enough to wander into Cell 45, she may find herself groped and scratched. If a woman is not unwary enough to wander into Cell 45, she may find herself inside it anyway, as people walking past the cell have at times been violently shoved forward through the doorway.

Still, angry, violent, loudmouth criminals are exactly what you'd expect to find haunting a historic gaol. As soon as you look at the old Geelong Gaol – and it is best viewed at night, to increase the sensation that you're at Arkham Asylum in a Batman film – you know that you're in for nasty ghosts with horrible pasts. Probably more upsetting than any of the hard cases, though, is the little girl you can see roaming around.

This proof of the axiom that little kids are the scariest thing in the world is a poignant relic of the period between 1865 and 1871, when the east wing of Geelong Gaol was converted into the Geelong Industrial School, where homeless girls were sent to live, a few feet away from murderers and rapists. The school was closed down after a report that described its record as 'many degrees worse than that of any other'. What fate befell the girl who now walks in the prison's halls, one shudders to think. And as for the source of the screams of young girls that occasionally emanate from the east wing – one is best advised not to think about that at all.

You can, if you wish, tour the old Geelong Gaol to see and hear and have your hair pulled for yourself; but there are few haunted spots in Australia less likely to be described as 'a bit of good harmless fun'. A history of blood and misery weighs the place down, and will likely weigh you down too.

The Black Hole

Albany, Western Australia

The current proprietors of the Albany Convict Gaol have, in the interests of giving their customers value for money in the frights department, adorned the rooms of the old building with a variety of dummies of frankly nightmarish aspect. They sit them in chairs to stare at you so that when you turn to go into a room, you jump out of your skin and let out an embarrassingly high-pitched noise because there's some kind of deformed evil gypsy watching you with one bulging eye.

To fall back on oversized novelty witch dolls from a Hungarian market stall would seem to suggest a certain lack of confidence on the owners' part in the essential scariness of the gaol itself. Which is a shame, because even without horrific Baba Yaga mannequins, the Albany Convict Gaol has plenty to make your flesh try to escape from your skeleton.

It was built, as the name suggests, in Albany, as a gaol for convicts. 'Aren't all gaols for convicts?' you may ask, but that's just you being snarky, because you know full well that what I mean is it was built to accommodate convicts sent to Albany as skilled labourers. That is, it was a gaol for the kind of convicts you learned about in third grade, not the ones you learn about at twenty-two when you fall in with the wrong crowd. Opened in 1852, it became a public prison in 1873, a police lockup in 1930 and a museum in 1996, whereupon the buildings were returned to their original state – except for the addition of the dummies.

Throughout the gaol can be heard the sounds of unhappy prisoners: a baby's cry often emanates from the women's cells, where a young woman died in childbirth. Elsewhere, the clanking of chains and the sound of whistling, as the inmates go about their daily work, could freeze you in your tracks, unless you allow yourself to feel a healthy appreciation for their work ethic.

One cell once held Frederick Bailey Deeming, who stopped over in Albany on his way to Melbourne to hang for the murder of his two wives and four children.* Some think Deeming was actually Jack the Ripper, although back in 1892 you could say that about almost anyone. Those who have entered Deeming's old cell have felt a disturbing presence and someone's hand on their heads. Which could be quite nice really, if the hand is sort of stroking you softly. But it probably isn't.

But the most horrific part of the Albany Convict Gaol is the one bound to petrify without the aid of any dummies – in fact, just hearing about it is usually enough to make a person shiver. This is the Black Hole: eight feet by four feet of solid stone, with no windows. This was where badly behaved convicts were placed for a punishment that could literally drive a man mad. On one occasion, twenty drunken soldiers were forced sardine-style into it for twenty-four hours: imagine that and see if your throat doesn't feel like closing over. Three of the soldiers died, and to this day horrible wails can be heard from the Black Hole, the hideous echoes of dying men's desperate pleas for salvation. Not that you need to hear wails in order for the Black Hole to horrify: a few seconds in the room is enough for a visitor to be overwhelmed by panic without any ghostly interference. It may be the best place in Australia to gain true empathy for the living hell that was convict life in the 1800s.

With the Black Hole in its repertoire, it's truly a mystery why the current management of the Albany Convict Gaol felt it necessary to install their community of horrid dummies. Though it's safer not to ask them about it, in case they say something awful, like, 'What dummies?'

---

* Talk about an excessive personality.

Steiglitz

Steiglitz, Victoria

The tiny town of Steiglitz lies in the Brisbane Ranges in southern Victoria, a confusing fact that proves yet again the necessity of a wider variety of placenames in Australia. As of 2015, the town had an official population of eight, making it not so much a town as a dinner party. But it was not always so: in 1863 the population of Steiglitz was over 2000, when prospectors had flooded the area. How sad the citizens of the bustling goldfields town would have been back then, had they known that one day their thriving home would suffer the cruellest fate for any town: becoming a historical park.

When Steiglitz was running hot as a goldfield, all was well. Compared to other fields, the gold was easy to extract: you could practically scoop it up off the ground. In the town's four pubs, the prospectors spent both their savings and their findings on the sweet nectar that made life worth living. In its three schools, children were taught to, for god's sake, not go to the four pubs. And in the old courthouse, the odd case of theft, assault and battery, or racially motivated gang violence against the Chinese community, was dealt with firmly but kindly, because everyone knew it was all in good fun. It was the kind of town Disney could've made a movie about with only minimal sanitising.

But though the gold was easy to get, it wasn't as plentiful as everyone had assumed. Like most gold-rush towns, Steiglitz had staked its future on the status quo continuing forever. Pickings became slim. Many packed up and left. Those who remained grew increasingly desperate as they tried to squeeze just a little more gold out of the barren ground. Pubs and schools closed, and the town's good nature began to sour.

It was then that dark deeds began to dominate in Steiglitz. With the flow of riches slowed to a trickle, what little could be found was guarded jealously, and sought even more jealously. Miners fought and stole from each other. Blood was spilled on the goldfields, picks and shovels finding unlucky skulls.

The walk from the town along Stawell Street to Sutherland Creek is these days known as Deadmans Loop, with good reason. More than a few drunken miners ended their days in that creek, either stumbling in or being deposited there.

All in all, in its progress from boom town to ghost town, Steiglitz lost its boisterous frontier character and became a grim and violent place. Today, the echoes of that violence are to be found in the spirits that appear around the town. In great numbers, the ghosts mass in the town, wandering the main street in search of a drink at one of the pubs that are no longer there. Down by the creek the spirits keep panning for gold, and out on the fields they keep digging, looking for the big score.

You'll meet these lost souls if you head out to Steiglitz and wait till sundown. For the town has no electricity, and when it gets dark … it gets really, *really* dark. And in the complete and utter inky blackness of a Steiglitz night, what remains of generations of unlucky prospectors past will show you that, up till now, you only *thought* you knew what 'ghost town' meant.

The Gravedigger's Cottage

Manly, New South Wales

The North Head Quarantine Station on Sydney Harbour hasn't been used for its original purpose for many years. The complex, now dubbed Q Station, houses a hotel, restaurant and function centre, and the more disturbing aspects of its past are just more fodder for the cracking good time to be had there. For example, you can go on a ghost tour, which will take you through the unimposing little old white house dubbed the Gravedigger's Cottage, of which one appreciative customer was heard to say, 'This place is pure evil.' Doesn't that entice you to book your holiday today?

The Gravedigger's Cottage never actually housed a gravedigger. It provided accommodation for doctors caring for the people stuck in the quarantine station until they could either be proven disease-free and released into the community or proven dead and released into the cemeteries.

There were two of these cemeteries, and the Gravedigger's Cottage is situated right between them, which is how it got its name. It's not the most cheerful place for a dwelling to be located, but at least it would have kept the doctors' minds focused on the job at hand.

But what's strange – and by strange, I mean seriously messed up – is that although there was no gravedigger resident in the Gravedigger's Cottage back when the quarantine station was operational, it seems as if there's one there *now*. At least, they call him the Gravedigger, and he's certainly dressed for the job: a long black cloak and a wide-brimmed black hat. He's been seen in the cottage, lurking in the darkness with eyes aglow.

If all that Q Station had to offer was the ghost of a sinister man in black in a cottage situated between two cemeteries, frankly, that would be enough. But the Gravedigger's Cottage has a lot more to offer anyone who steps through its doors.

The bathroom, for example, has been called the most haunted in Sydney, and not just because, with its pink walls and light-green bath and sink, it appears to have been decorated by a psychopath. It is believed that, long ago, a woman was murdered in the cottage: drowned in the bath. Over the years, thousands have passed through the building and felt the homicidal energy in the air. There is death within its walls, and the reverberations of dreadful deeds.

People have suffered panic attacks in the Gravedigger's Cottage. People have fainted right away. People have reported feeling the floorboards shifting and rising beneath their feet, and a prickly heat all over that makes them desperate to flee the place. But there's worse to be experienced, under the watchful eye of the Gravedigger.

There are those who have felt invisible fingers close around their throats, and invisible hands pressing on their chests, trying to force them down. Some have said, as they feel themselves being pushed down and the floor rising up to meet them, that suddenly it seems as if their head has been submerged underwater. It would appear that whoever committed that dreadful murder in the cottage's bathroom is still around, and still looking for victims to drown.

So oppressive is the atmosphere, and so extreme the physical effects felt by visitors to the cottage, that the operators of the Q Station ghost tours don't always include it: they'll skip the Gravedigger's portion of the tour if they feel the party is on the fragile side. Not that there aren't sufficient scares throughout the rest of the old station: a sinister figure stalks the nurses' quarters, and throughout the grounds there is the ever-present risk of being groped by the ghost of a mortician called Mr Slimey.

But these are trifles compared to the dark power of the Gravedigger's Cottage, where whoever and whatever dwells there is determined to make everyone who drops by have the worst night of their life.

The Madman of Boggo Road

Dutton Park, Queensland

There have been stories of ghosts at the old Boggo Road Gaol – its official name is Brisbane Gaol, but it's been dubbed Boggo Road because the road it's on was known for its appalling conditions since the 1930s – although it's hard to tell what's true and what was a deliberate prank being played by the ever-jocular staff. Officer Ron Darby used to ride a bike around the gaol with a sheet over his head, which most would say was not the behaviour of a stable man, but perhaps that's simply evidence of the terrible toll the corrections system can take on the mental health of its employees, and not of paranormal activity. Nevertheless, the tales have persisted: a mysterious woman appearing on the upper floors; invisible inmates whispering in ears; and Tripod the three-legged cat, who meows and rubs himself on visitors' legs. Tripod supposedly can't be seen, so how anyone knows he has three legs is a mystery, but such is often the way with ghosts.

But such stories pale – even paler than normal – into insignificance when put up against Boggo Road's most notorious resident: Ernie.

Ernest Austin was twenty-two when in 1913 he was hanged at Boggo Road Gaol for the murder of eleven-year-old Ivy Mitchell. Ivy had disappeared while walking home from a friend's house. Her body was found in the scrub behind the local school, lying beside a bag of lollies and a bunch of flowers that she had picked that day. She had been raped and her throat slashed.

Austin, a local farmhand, was quickly tracked down and arrested. It was discovered that in 1909 he'd served three years in prison in Melbourne after dragging a twelve-year-old girl into a shed while carrying an axe. Back then, Austin had run off, in fear of the girl's screams attracting attention, before he could carry out the job as he would four years later with Ivy Mitchell.

Austin's hanging was the last to be carried out in Queensland, which abolished the death penalty in 1922. Accounts of his execution varied: newspaper reports had it that he walked calmly to the gallows, quietly accepting his fate. 'I hope you will forgive me,' he was reported as saying. 'I hope you will all live long and die happy – warders and all. God be with you.'

That's if you believe the press, which as we all know you should never do. If you accept the account of Austin's fellow inmates at Boggo Road, the hanging played out somewhat differently. For they say Austin, a madman to the end, laughed hysterically as the hangman slipped the noose over his head.

It's impossible to tell which execution story is the true one, but let's be honest: we want it to be the one where Austin is a cackling maniac, and it's perfectly reasonable to assume it is. Especially given that, in the century or so since his death, he's not shown an enormous amount of remorse, and no desire at all that anyone live long and die happy.

In fact, late at night, when the skies are stormy, Ernie is said to come out, drifting through brick walls and steel doors. When the gaol was still in operation, he would sneak into the cells of his fellow prisoners, falling upon them in their sleep and trying to strangle them. Many convicts awoke with a start, gasping and scrabbling at the invisible hands around their necks.

These days, of course, there are no convicts at Boggo Road, so it's the guests of ghost tours that Ernie likes to seize upon. Sightseers and tourists now know the feeling of the crazed killer's hands grabbing at them as they walk the prison halls. There's no danger, of course:

Ernie's dead and can't hurt anyone now. There's simply the harmless knowledge that in the vast, echoing spaces of the empty gaol, the spirit of a psychotic child killer is lying in wait. Which is, obviously, nothing to be afraid of.

The Howling at Camp Quaranup

Albany, Western Australia

Camp Quaranup, which sounds like a great name for one of those camps in American movies that are made to try to convince the rest of the world that sending your children away to be cared for by irresponsible teenagers for three months every year is a real thing that people in America do, isn't actually that. What it is is an old quarantine station at Albany, Western Australia, and it gets its name from combining 'quarantine' – the purpose for which it was built – with 'up' – the direction in which you have to walk to get there from the bottom of the hill.

Camp Quaranup was established to house sick people who came to Western Australia trying to cough on the locals. The necessity for a quarantine station at Albany was made clear after a group of dignitaries were forced to quarantine in tents in the rain on Mistaken Island, which got its name from the fact that it was located in the middle of a field.[*] A proper facility was demanded and so the station was built, and from then on, instead of being let loose to spread disease, travellers would be shut up in Quaranup until they either got better or died – the

---

[*] Mistaken Island was actually, no joke, named after the fact that the first Europeans who visited it thought the burrows of the fairy penguins were rabbit holes. Could've called it Penguin Island or Burrow Island, but nup.

administration weren't all that fussed which.

As things panned out, a hell of a lot of people *did* die at the quarantine station, but this was no surprise at all – in the 19th century, people could generally be expected to drop like flies simply out of a sense of historical continuity, so when they were crammed together into a confined space to share diseases, it was absolute carnage. Later on, the station became a submarine base, which was not as interesting as it sounds. Today it actually *is* a holiday camp, although it should be stressed that it's not one to which you may send your children to be cared for by teenagers.

The supernatural shenanigans associated with Quaranup can be traced back to the quarantine days – or at least one assumes so, given that none of the ghosts appears to be a naval officer. One of the most prominent, in fact, is a little girl, and even in the most desperate days of the Second World War, those weren't allowed to serve in submarines.

The little girl of Quaranup wanders the camp grounds in a Victorian-era nightgown. She seems lost, perhaps searching for her parents who have succumbed to smallpox, or just looking for the toilets. In just that nightgown, and wearing no shoes, it's a worry that she might catch her death – which in all likelihood she did. The child seems to have no particular aim except to creep you out by being a freaky little girl, but that's quite enough.

But the most famous of Quaranup's current residents – the star of the show, as it were – is the phantom howler. This is the ghost of a young man whose body was found underneath one of the quarantine station's buildings. He had been electrocuted, apparently having tangled with the house's wiring a little too closely – an excellent cautionary tale.

Today that unfortunate man, like his young female colleague, also wanders the camp grounds, but somewhat more ostentatiously. For it's said that every night, as he roams around the camp, he *howls*.

Now, that's pretty wild, right? He doesn't moan, like a ghost. He doesn't even scream, like a spirit reliving the horror of his own death. No, he *howls*. Like a werewolf. There is something distinctly disturbing about this, even by ghost standards. Maybe the howl is the sound he made as the lethal jolt of electricity shot through him. Maybe it's simply a howl of anguish at the incorporeal circumstances he's found himself in. Maybe he actually is the ghost of a werewolf, but because he died in human form he doesn't get to transform as a ghost, and is just frustrated as hell.

Whatever the case, if you can say that you, on a holiday to Camp Quaranup, could be awakened from your slumber by the seaside, in the place where once the afflicted died in their dozens, by the sound of a ghostly young man howling in the darkness, and not soil yourself in terror … well, frankly, you're just lying.

The Blue Nun of New Norcia

New Norcia, Western Australia

Sister Maria Harispe came to New Norcia, 132 kilometres north of Perth, from Paraguay in 1907. She was twenty-six years old and had come to Australia to give the local Aboriginal people a good Christian education. This was, of course, a horrible thing to do to them, but Sister Maria didn't know that at the time, and all indications are that she meant well. In fact, she grew to love the Indigenous people of New Norcia and dedicated the rest of her life to their welfare.

New Norcia is Australia's only monastic town, founded in 1847 by Spanish Benedictine monks who believed the local Yued population could be converted to Christianity, which, again, was a pretty awful thing to want to do, despite their noble intentions. When Sister Maria arrived, she went to work at St Joseph's Native School and Orphanage, which was run by Benedictine missionary sisters from Spain. From 1908 she ran the school, becoming a beloved figure in the community. Whatever the merits or otherwise of the colonial urge to convert everyone to Christianity, Sister Maria's love for and devotion to the children at St Joseph's could never be doubted.

In 1925, Sister Maria sadly fell victim to cancer, dying in November at the age of forty-four. The church bells tolled the news of her passing, and the people gathered around the abbey church to pray. 'She was a mother to everyone,' said one New Norcia local, 'so we were without a mother.' Although the good sister died young, she died just where she had wanted to: among the Yued people, whom she considered to be her family.

The town was bereft, but the work of the orphanage and school went on, and with time it seems that its beloved principal had not let death prevent her from continuing to oversee its operations.

For nearly a century now, since Sister Maria departed, the folk of New Norcia have reported the eerie, yet oddly reassuring sight of a nun at the old clock tower of the abbey church. This is the site of the tomb of Dom Rosendo Salvado, one of the two Spanish monks who founded New Norcia, and a sacred place for the Benedictine order. If it is to be haunted, it is only right that it be haunted by the woman whose devotion to the work of the order was so deep and passionate.

She wears a blue habit when making her rounds and she appears every night when the clock in the tower strikes midnight. She wanders the tower and, according to some accounts, occasionally takes flight and makes an aerial circuit.

A ghost in a clock tower can be an unnerving thing: a lot of nasty business has been known to go on in and around clock towers, and a spectre being in one naturally raises questions about what horror was done to bring it about. But there is nothing malevolent about the Blue Nun: Sister Maria is in death as she was in life: a spirit of love and caring. All she wants – all she ever wanted – is to keep watch over her town and her people. And what better place to do that than from the clock tower?

St Joseph's is no longer an orphanage: it has become the New Norcia Museum and Art Gallery, the home of the Mandorla Art Award, the only Australian award for artworks based on Christian scriptural themes. One assumes that the Blue Nun approves.

Z Ward

Adelaide, South Australia

Asylums. It always comes back to asylums somehow. The Parkside Lunatic Asylum in Adelaide was opened in 1870, catering to all those who found the stress of being South Australian just too much to bear. The building was designed in the Gothic Revival style, to make sure that everyone who saw it realised that it was a spooky asylum, and until 1973 it operated basically as a ghost factory, churning out unhappy, lost souls by the dozen.

Like anywhere that ever had 'Lunatic Asylum' in its name, the methods at Parkside were appalling, and its staff were both cruel and completely lacking in qualifications. And also like anywhere bearing such a title, it is now turning a nice profit for ghost-tour operators. 'Can you spend five minutes in the dark, in a small cell, on your own?' asks the advertising for these tours, to which the answer is, 'Yes – but what sort of idiot would want to?'

The place to be, should you be in the market to descend into a nightmarish world of madness and horror, is Z Ward. This was the ward at Parkside reserved for the criminally insane: so the ghosts here aren't just distressed and unstable, they really want to hurt people. The danger posed by some of the inmates is indicated by the fact that the asylum is surrounded by a ha-ha. A ha-ha, of course, being a form of fortification dating back to medieval times, whereby a wall is set in a sunken ditch so as to hide it from view. It's also quite an insensitive thing to build around a mental health institution.

Deep within the ha-ha lurk myriad unhappy spirits. Walking through Z Ward, one is liable to come into contact with them in a very tactile way. Guests have reported arms being grabbed, backs being patted and heads being pushed, as the restless Z Ward ghosts delight in having some real live people to touch and feel. In Scratchy's Room, they go even further. Unfortunately, the room did not get its name due to any kind of *Simpsons*-themed decor: entrants to Scratchy's have found angry red marks spontaneously appearing on their skin, as if they've been savaged by long claws.

In the Mirror Room, on the other hand, the scars left are more likely to be psychological. As the name suggests, this room contains a mirror, and that mirror contains one of the tortured wretches who never left Parkside alive. Wreathed in shadow, he appears in the glass to stare out with wild, haunted eyes.

And then there's Room 2. Very little information is available about Room 2, except that the operators of the Z Ward ghost tours don't let anyone go in there alone. What dwells in there remains, for anyone who's yet to enter it, a mystery. But given its location in a place whose history is drenched with pain and torment and misery, where some of the most violent and irredeemable criminals were housed, and where vulnerable people were abused, subjected to horrific experimental treatments, and often outright murdered, and given that this room is apparently even worse than the others … well, feel free to use your imagination. Suffice it to say nobody comes out of Room 2 with an enviable equilibrium.

Sometimes a ghost will be seen walking through Z Ward, but mostly its phantoms prefer to steer away from full-body apparitions. Feeling the hands grab you, the nails scratch you, catching a glimpse of a tormented face in a mirror … they prefer to operate in these less obvious ways. Perhaps because, being trapped in a madhouse themselves, their main aim is to drive anyone else who comes inside mad as well. Take up the challenge to spend five minutes alone in the dark in one of the cells, and it's entirely possible they'll get their wish.

Ghosts of the Gaiety

Zeehan, Tasmania

Some might say that a place named the Gaiety Theatre doesn't sound like the kind of place to be crammed full of ghosts. What bigoted thinkers those people are: who says ghosts can't be gay, in either the archaic or the modern sense?

Of course, it's in the former sense that the Gaiety Theatre was named, back in 1898, as back then men's collars were far too stiff to allow homosexuality. One showed one's affection for one's fellow man with a firm and masculine handshake, and never kissed a chap unless you were cradling him as he died in battle.

The Gaiety Theatre is located in Zeehan, on the west coast of Tasmania, and for a time early in its history it achieved the almost unheard-of feat of attracting visitors to Zeehan. Harry Houdini himself once walked a tightrope from the Gaiety's balcony across the main street in a display that really does give credence to the rumours that he was a bit of a show-off – but it drew a crowd.

Houdini was a great sceptic, of course, and when he wasn't walking tightropes, escaping from boxes or being surprised by men punching him in the stomach before he was ready, he devoted much energy to debunking claims of paranormal activity. He would no doubt be disappointed, therefore, were he to discover that his one-time stamping ground in Zeehan was today the site of ghost tours and rumours of hauntings. However, if Houdini was correct about the supernatural being nonsense, then he's long dead and has no way of knowing about it, so that's convenient. If by any chance the ghost of Houdini were to turn up at the Gaiety Theatre, it would be incredibly embarrassing for everyone.

Another prominent performer to grace the Gaiety's stage was Dame Nellie Melba, but she already has a haunting gig at Melbourne's Hotel Windsor and presumably can't be bothered hanging around in Zeehan. The ghosts of the Gaiety are far humbler folk, though no less worthy for it. They simply want to know that the history of the old theatre is not forgotten, and that the economy of Tasmania's west coast is thriving on the back of tourists coming to the Gaiety to be scared.

Today, the Gaiety houses the Grand Hotel, as well as screening movies. The days of sixty-strong revues playing to 1000-strong crowds are over, but the remnants of those who worked at the theatre back then can still be seen and heard pottering around behind the scenes. Stagehands haul on invisible ropes, managers stroll briskly about backstage, ticket-sellers wait alertly for custom. You have to be quick to catch them: they flicker in and out of view when the lights are low, drifting in and out of the mortal realm at those points where the boundary between it and the other-world starts to fray.

The best known and most seen of the Gaiety's cast of spirits is Ava, the theatre's proud addition to the pantheon of unsettling little-girl ghosts. Ava was the daughter of a caretaker at the Gaiety: a caretaker who apparently could not organise adequate childcare, because he kept bringing young Ava to work to hang around the theatre – and hang around she has, for a century or more. How she met her end is uncertain: possibly an accident with a curtain or a trapdoor. Or maybe she lived a long and full life, died an old lady and just decided that the most satisfying way to spend the eternity of death was as a nine-year-old skipping around the old theatre she used to love so well. It'd be nice to think so, although it's definitely more likely that something fell on her head.

If you visit the Gaiety Theatre today, there's a fair chance you'll spot Ava scurrying about. She won't pay you any attention: there are far more interesting things going on at the Gaiety than tourism.

Winston of Ward 5

New Norfolk, Tasmania

Determining whether the Royal Derwent Hospital, popularly known as Willow Court, is haunted is a relatively simple process. Just ask the question, 'Is Willow Court Australia's oldest mental health facility?' If the answer is 'yes', then OF COURSE IT'S HAUNTED, YOU IDIOT. I mean, surely we know by now: if it's old and it once housed the mentally ill, there will be ghosts fizzing about inside it.

Willow Court was founded in 1827 as an 'invalid depot'. The Governor of Van Diemen's Land, George Arthur, then decreed that he would 'concentrate all lunatics at New Norfolk,'* and the institution became known as the New Norfolk Lunatic Asylum. A desire to not injure the patients' self-esteem while performing horrifically abusive procedures on them saw it renamed the New Norfolk Hospital for the Insane, then the Mental Diseases Hospital, then Lachlan Park Hospital, then finally the Royal Derwent Hospital. Throughout all the name changes, one thing has remained constant: marrow-freezing terror.

In the asylum's abortion chair – and isn't that a cheery phrase – there is a spirit called Sarah, who seems bound to that spot forever. In the morgue is the spirit of a quite unpleasant doctor, who will touch your legs and neck if you lie on the slab. In Ward C, red hand marks

---

*   It sounds unfeasible, but there were a lot fewer lunatics in Tasmania back then than there are now, so they had room.

have appeared on clothes and couldn't be washed out. And then there is Winston.

Winston dwelled in Ward 5 of the old asylum, and he is not happy. Mediums who have entered the ward have determined that Winston is his name, but he is also known as the Male-Hating Ghost, as he has a habit of attacking male members of staff. Where Winston came from is unknown: some say the ward used to house young drug addicts who dabbled in the occult; others claim that the staff held a seance in the ward one night and were interrupted, leaving the door to the Other Side open. One way or another, Winston got into Ward 5 and has repeatedly shown himself to be displeased with his lot.

Numerous staff at the asylum reported seeing Winston: he took the form of a white haze, sometimes with a torso and head, and would follow people down halls and into rooms. At times on the ward were heard the sounds of feet scuffing along corridors, and something being dragged along the floor. Music would play from nowhere, and the smell of bread being toasted would fill the air in the middle of the night.

On one terrifying occasion, a nurse discovered one of his colleagues in the office in Ward 5, lying on the floor, thrashing about and clutching at his throat. When the victim spoke, it was not in his own voice, but a deep growl. In that growl, he begged, 'Get it out of me, get it out of me!'

A similar tale was told by another staff member: they saw a white film appear behind a colleague, who suddenly fell to the floor, grabbing his throat and writhing desperately. 'It feels like something is inside me,' said the second member of staff.

Winston's attacks became so serious that the hospital appealed to the Catholic Church to perform an exorcism, to which the Catholic Church replied that that isn't how exorcisms work, and maybe read a book once in a while, huh?*

Most of the sightings of Winston were quite indistinct: bright lights, hazes or films, which sometimes took a vaguely human shape. One

---

* Exorcisms are for people who have demons inside them, not for ghosts who get frisky now and then.

patient on Ward 5, however, saw Winston in a far more explicit form. In her own words: 'I lived on Ward 5, there was a ghost on Ward 5. I saw the ghost, he wore a black coat, white shirt and black trousers, he smoked a pipe. He was scary.'

Ward 5 has since been demolished – a sound idea, to be honest – but on the grounds where it once stood, many have reported that Winston's presence seems to remain.

The Poinciana Woman

East Point, Northern Territory

It was at East Point Reserve, where today children play and families lay out picnics – and where, during the Second World War, great guns stood to defend the country from the threat from the north. It was at that green and pleasant spot, in hot and balmy Darwin, that the woman was caught beneath the Poinciana tree by wicked men. It was there that she was beaten and raped by the monsters; when they were done, they strung her up from the branch of the poinciana tree. It was there she was found the next day, hanging lifeless among the flame flowers.

They never knew who she was, the poor woman caught beneath the poinciana tree. Nor did they know who the wicked men were who had pounced on her and destroyed her. She died alone and friendless, her screams bringing no assistance and her tears drawing no mercy. They cut her down from the poinciana tree and buried her, and then forgot her and moved on with their lives.

But the Poinciana Woman did not move on. She did not go away. She did not forget.

She wanders there still, beneath the poinciana tree at East Point Reserve, walking in the night and brooding on the outrage that was committed against her. You can summon her if you wish, if you stand by the tree on a moonless night and spin round three times while calling

266

out her name.* Then she will appear to you, and you will soon discover whether you are to regret your decision to call to her.

Because to some she is an angel of mercy, and to others ...

It is said that she waits on the other side of the wall between this world and the next, and welcomes those women who have died in childbirth, bringing comfort to their restless souls. To these unfortunates she is kind and loving.

But she has quite a different face when she emerges from the darkness and stalks the reserve. For then, it is said, she walks in search of revenge. To men, she will appear as she once was: a beautiful young woman, dressed all in white, shining in the dark and beckoning her quarry to her. Such a vision is not to be resisted: the reckless man will go to her, and reach out, beneath the poinciana tree ...

And it is then the vision cracks and warps, and the fair maiden in the white dress transforms into a horror from hell: a wild-eyed witch with a bristling shock of hair flying behind her in the sudden wind, and long, razor-sharp talons on each hand that take hold of the unwary fellow, slashing and tearing and pulling him to pieces.

The Poinciana Woman's scream on these moonless nights can be heard across the fields, like the dreadful call of a monstrous bird, as she seizes her prey, rips his body open and feeds on his guts. She will scream again and again, in triumph, her revenge well taken. She will then melt away into the black night, temporarily sated but already preparing for her return, to once again wreak vengeance on men.

So anyone seeking an audience with the Poinciana Woman needs to be fully prepared: if you are a woman, she may well greet you cheerfully; if you are a man, she will greet you with a smile too – at which point you should run as far and as fast as you can from the flame tree and the flowers that burn in the night.

Is the Poinciana Woman real? Perhaps. Or maybe it's just a story. There are lots of tales flying about the world, and not all of them can be

---

* Of course, we don't know what her name is, making this tricky and calling into doubt the practicality of urban legends as a guide to meaningful action.

true. Maybe there was no woman, no wicked men, no outrage under the bright red blossoms. Maybe there is no spectre looming beneath the poinciana tree to avenge her brutal end.

In which case, you're perfectly safe, so why not head out to East Point Reserve, find that tree and turn around three times …

Norfolklore

Kingston, Norfolk Island

In the 19th century, the penal settlement at Norfolk Island gained a reputation as the place to send convicts when Port Arthur was deemed too cushy for them. Being a distant island that had yet to develop any sort of sophisticated cafe culture, Norfolk was the ideal place to dispatch people for whom you considered hanging too good. The idea was that if men were sent to Australia as punishment but kept on misbehaving, they would be moved on to Norfolk Island – in the same way that if you've already grounded your children but they still won't do as they're told, you can run over them in your car.

This wasn't really how it played out, though: plenty of convicts were shipped off to Norfolk Island despite being non-violent and not particularly troublesome. Of course, they often became troublesome once they got there, as they kicked up a stink over being treated like animals – and not even animals that the government liked.

There were strong, rough men on Norfolk Island who openly wept when they were told they would not be hanged, for execution had been the only thing they had to look forward to. Given the dangerously high levels of unhappiness, and the limited life spans, it's no surprise that Norfolk today is swarming with ghosts who feel pretty hard done by. In fact, the island has more ghosts per square kilometre than any other state or territory in Australia, as measured by some people who do that sort of thing. Canadian website *The Paranormal* named Norfolk as the fourth-most-haunted island in the world, which we can only assume is pretty impressive.

On one occasion, a convict had hopes of escaping Norfolk and went down to the landing place at Kingston, the old capital of the island, to wait for a boat that would pick him up and whisk him to freedom. The vessel did approach, but the man had to swim out to it, and in the rough seas he drowned. Today, the ghost of the convict can be seen on the cliff above the landing place, staring out to sea, still hoping he will be picked up and taken the hell out of there. When you approach the vision, he disappears: he's in no mood for company.

There is an old cemetery at Kingston, full of unlucky folk who were crushed by Norfolk, and for many years it's been said that if you are walking past it at night, you need to whistle, to send the ghosts back to their graves. Why do the ghosts return to their graves after hearing a whistle? Scientists, sadly, have yet to find the answer to this.

More ghosts can be found on the road to the cable station, where they congregate in the same spot each evening when darkness falls. Whistling does no good to disperse these meetings, but if you just steer a wide berth around them you should be fine, as they've got their own business to conduct.

The most picturesque ghosts are to be found in the aptly named Quality Row, the Kingston street where most of the official houses were located and which was the centre of what passed for respectable society on Norfolk Island. Here the spirits put on a show worthy of any overpriced colonial theme park. Red-coated soldiers still march down the thoroughfare, rifles on shoulders, while ladies in long crinoline dresses twirl their parasols on the street. And all the while, the clink-clank-clink of the chain gangs echoes around the empty stone cottages. It's almost festive, in a way, if you can push to the back of your mind the knowledge that the men on the chain gang were probably near starvation and bleeding profusely from the whip.

Norfolk Island is today a gorgeous spot, a South Pacific idyll perfect for a holiday. The presence of a pile of ruins with a legacy of unspeakable cruelty is somewhat incongruous, but it does offer the chance to have a sunny island holiday while also meeting an array of interesting dead people – and how often do you get to do that?

Good Old Fred

Hobart, Tasmania

The theatre technician was halfway up the ladder onstage when he felt it. The hair on the back of his neck stood up. A shiver slithered its way through his body from top to tail. His knuckles turned white as he gripped the ladder with all his strength, suddenly possessed by an inexplicable feeling that he was about to fall. He slowly looked from left to right, afraid that even the movement of his eyes would cause him to lose his balance, yet simultaneously unable to resist the awful temptation to try to see who was watching him – for he could not be any more certain that someone was.

There was no one there. No one that he could see. But as he held on tight, flesh crawling, he heard a voice. As clear as if the speaker were standing right next to him, twenty feet above the stage. 'Why show here?' the voice asked. A second later, the air seemed to clear. The tech's neck hairs settled down. His grip relaxed. He resumed his climb. But the words kept reverberating in his brain. 'Why show here?'

The tech soon learned that there was nothing to fear: he had simply had a run-in with Fred, the kindly ghost of Hobart's Theatre Royal. From then on, when he was the first in to work he would say g'day to Fred, and if he was the last to leave he'd say goodbye, and Fred never caused him any problems again.

For Fred is no malevolent theatre phantom, terrorising staff and theatregoers. Rather, he is an easygoing old gent who feels strongly protective of the jewel in Hobart's theatrical crown. Every truly classy theatre needs a resident ghost, and Fred fits the bill nicely, serving more as a mascot than a horrifying apparition.

In the 19th century, Fred was an actor. Back then, a century before Errol Flynn got his big break, Tasmania was not the greatest place for an actor with ambition, and, like so many others, Fred found his career never broke out beyond the Apple Isle. To be fair, this may have had less to do with any lack of thespian talent – or even the absence of opportunity afforded to those at the furthest outposts of empire in a world without mass global communication networks – than with the fact that, when he was still quite young, Fred picked a fight with another actor, who ended up killing him.

This was a real bugger, but it's testament to Fred's positive attitude that he has never let his untimely death get him down.* Instead, he simply moved onto a new stage in his existence: as overseer of the Theatre Royal. Mostly this is fairly mundane work: late at night, when performances are over, he goes about telling people to go home – which can be a little startling the first time it happens to you, but be assured that Fred's only concern is for the orderly running of the theatre, and his desire that you should not miss the last bus home. But there was one occasion on which Fred went above and beyond to protect his beloved place of work.

It was 1984, by which time the theatre was 147 years old. Fred was even older. There may have been a carelessly dropped cigarette or an electrical malfunction, but whatever it was, it caused a fire to roar to life inside the building. The blaze grew quickly with nobody there to quell it, and the Theatre Royal was in genuine danger of burning to the ground. A hundred and forty-seven years of history up in smoke – but then, enter Fred.

In the absence of corporeal assistance, the resident ghost stepped in and stepped up. Acting with commendable coolness under pressure,

---

* Well, he probably did a little bit. On the day it happened, at least.

despite the escalating temperature, Fred quickly dropped the theatre's fire curtain onto the growing blaze, snuffing it out in one fell swoop.

The Theatre Royal had been saved by a ghost, and that ghost could be assured of an honoured place in his old haunt forevermore.

The Coach & Horses

Clarkefield, Victoria

On the north-west fringe of Melbourne, in the shadow of the Macedon Ranges, lies Clarkefield, a quiet little suburb generally overlooked. It is a place to which the adjective 'remarkable' can be accurately applied but rarely, although it does have one claim to fame among lovers of the eldritch and supernatural: the Coach & Horses Inn.

It is a charming bluestone building on Station Street, with vintage fixtures providing old-world atmosphere in the public bar, and a good parma to be had in the bistro. It is also one of the most haunted pubs in the world, and has a history of ghosts both lively and mischievous that has attracted many curious visitors over the years, while frightening off those of a less inquisitive bent.

It seems that the Coach & Horses has that peculiar ability of some buildings to bind the spirits of those who pass through it – particularly if they were unlucky enough to end their days on the premises. One young Irishman named Patrick Reagan, a goldminer who'd checked in to the inn to enjoy some of the spoils of his diggings, was robbed and shot dead out the front. For many years after his death, stories were told by those who saw Reagan running frantically up the pub stairs, still trying to escape the thugs who did him in.

They've also seen the ghost of a Chinese man, loitering mournfully around the hotel. This is another unhappy former miner, who got himself into a fight that proved well beyond his ability to get out of, with the end result that his antagonists hanged him in the stables.

In the toilets of the pub, children visiting with their families have seen and heard a little girl crying. This poor child, around eight years old, once was believed to have been killed at the Coach & Horses, but her body was later found in a well nearby, apparently the victim of a terrible accident. Her ghost hangs around the tavern seemingly not to scare anyone, but simply to find someone to play with: she cries because she is lonely, but reacts with delight when she finds new young friends.

One couple who took over the inn in the 1980s quickly sold it again after seeing the ghost of the girl, hearing inexplicable footsteps at night and seeing paintings on the walls shifting from their places. Another former proprietor of the establishment had no fear of ghosts until he was awoken one night by the rattling of bottles and glasses. Heading downstairs, he was struck by a cold breeze and then an invisible presence, which shoved him down the stairs, breaking his foot in three places.

In the early days of Clarkefield, the Coach & Horses would have served as a makeshift morgue, keeping corpses found in the town in its coolroom. Like other haunted country pubs, it's possible that its battalion of ghosts is a result of this: so many dead bodies spent time in the pub that a decent number released their immortal souls into the ether there. And in such an exciting variety of forms: the full-body apparitions of the young girl and the murdered Irishman mix with the poltergeists pushing people down stairs and chucking paintings around; as well as a worrying man's face that appears on a tree in the garden, and an ineffable presence that periodically causes animals in the vicinity to start acting up. Things that go bump in the night are common, and bright, glowing figures move about the building in the small hours.

Long may the Coach & Horses Inn stand proud on Station Street, serving the people of Clarkefield and those just passing through between the city and the mountains. Otherwise, the day it falls, its many ghosts will be rendered homeless.

The Bushranger Hotel

Collector, New South Wales

Just off the Federal Highway, north of Lake George, lies the little town of Collector. It was hereabouts, in 1865, that Ben Hall and his gang rode into town after bailing up travellers on the road to Goulburn. While in Collector, Hall went into a local pub, Kimberley's Commercial Hotel, taking guns, boots and clothing from it. As the bushrangers tarried, local constable Samuel Nelson hurried to the hotel to confront them – alone, outnumbered and, as it turned out, extremely unwisely. His devotion to duty was to cost him when Hall's teenage sidekick, John Dunn, gunned him down in the road outside.

It's thanks to this infamous incident that Kimberley's Commercial Hotel came to be known as the Bushranger Hotel, forevermore carrying the powerful whiff of history and bloodshed in its walls. It can be an unnerving place to visit, with its stuffed kangaroo and snakes in jars providing an authentic atmosphere of whatever the hell stuffed kangaroos and snakes in jars are supposed to conjure up.

The Bushranger Hotel becomes even more unnerving when you get to grips – or not, as the case may be – with some of its more venerable residents. Bushrangers no longer hang out in the bar, but there are plenty of folks from times long past inhabiting the premises. The thud of heavy boots is oftentimes heard passing through the doorways, while figures of wispy white are seen drifting in and out of the rooms. Women who have stayed at the pub have felt their hair being stroked, ghostly fingers running lovingly through their locks. Such attentions may not have met with universal approval.

In the kitchen of the Bushranger, pots and pans are frequently hurled about the place when nobody is there, while taps turn off and on without warning, and strange shadows appear and disappear in mirrors. In the middle of the night, the publican says, one can feel trapped: the air of the hotel presses in around you, paralyses you as you feel an overwhelming urge to run, but can't.

The most prominent member of the Bushranger Hotel community is Jimmy Quirk, one-time publican, who still dwells in the hotel with his son. In fact, the Quirks don't just dwell: they keep doing their job just as they did many years ago. Glasses slide around under invisible hands on top of the bar. Sometimes a Bushranger employee leaves the room and returns to find empty glasses cleaned and neatly stacked. And, of course, no bartender is perfect: sometimes glasses fall and break out of nowhere.

There have been several guests who have come to stay at the Bushranger, only to change their minds rapidly. After spending a little time in their room, they refuse to stay the night and leave in a panicked hurry. It's hard to blame them, as there is a presence in the pub that clearly militates against a good night's rest. But if the Bushranger Hotel is not a great place to stay, it's still a great place to work: even death doesn't stop the staff coming in for their shift. You've got to admire a workplace culture like that.

Acknowledgements

As always, a great many people are owed tremendous thanks for their part in making this book possible. To begin with, the lovely folk at Affirm Press, especially Armelle Davies, Martin Hughes and Coco McGrath, who helped shepherd the fledgling tome – can fledglings be shepherded? Anyway – from conception to completion.

Massive gratitude must go to Les, Helen and Alice Pobjie, Rebecca Davis and Emily Maguire, who all helped keep me alive throughout the writing, and Freda Stozki, who supported me even when I didn't.

Huge thanks to Campbell Smith, steadfast friend and comrade in arms, with whom I have discussed the nature and personalities of ghosts many times over the years and whose inspiration I continually draw on.

And huge thanks to Jay Freeman, for spiritual support and training in the art of storytelling.

But most of all I must thank all the ghosts of Australia, who, whether they exist or not, have done a sterling job of haunting, spooking and providing endless hours of entertainment to Australians of all ages. Thank you all – you've truly earned that eternal rest which, being ghosts, you will of course forever be denied.